HONEY,
I BLEW UP THE
KIDS!

Michael J. Lincoln, Ph.D.
1992, Revised 2007

HONEY, I BLEW UP THE KIDS!

Copyright © 1992 Michael J. Lincoln, Ph.D.,
2007 Revised Talking Hearts
All Rights Reserved

Published by Talking Hearts
Printed in the USA
2nd   Print 2007

ISBN: 0-9772069-2-0

For all U.S. and International book orders and consultations with
Michael J. Lincoln, Ph.D. visit our website at www.talkinghearts.net
or write to P.O. Box 194, Cool, CA 95614

Also by the Author:

Addictions and Cravings: Their Psychological Meaning (1991, Rev. 2006)
Allergies and Aversions: Their Psychological Meaning (1991, Rev. 2006)
Animals: Their Psycho-Symbolic Meaning (1991, Rev. 2007)
Healer's Handbook for Practitioners (from Messages from the Body (1991, Rev. 2006))
It's All in the Family: Exploration of the Life Scripts (1992, Rev. 2007)
Messages from the Body: Their Psychological Meaning (1991, Rev. 2006)
Problematic Patterns: Behavioral, Psychological and Psychiatric Problems-Their Emotional Meaning (1991, Rev. 2007)
What's Happening to ME!!?? The Roadmap to the Healing and Change Process (1981, Rev. 2007)
What's in a FACE? The Dictionary for Heart Centered Face Reading (1990, Rev. 2007)

Soon to be Revised and Expanded:

A Funny Thing Happened… On the Way to My Life
Clothes Consciousness
Household Hot Spots: Their Psycho-Symbolic Meaning – Utilitarian Meaning
Hue Are You?
Louder than Words: Behavior Reading
My Car, Myself
Nonverbal Messages
Speech Habits
What was THAT All About?!

For more information visit our website at www.talkinghearts.net
or write to P.O. Box 194, Cool, CA 95614

CONTENTS

INTRODUCTION

This is a book about the parenting process -- what's involved, what's needed and what we know about it. It is composed of a series of essays. In general, this is not a "how to" book on how to go about the day-to-day management of the requirements on parenting.

It is instead a primer on how to *approach* the parenting process. It lays out a general framework for understanding what your child(ren) are doing and what you are doing as you go about living with, rearing, and launching your child(ren).

The whole thing is really about facilitating the destinies that your children come in with. This means that every interaction every day is about meeting the child's needs in a manner that they can then carry out the purposes that they came here with.

Because the topic is so huge and so multi-facetted, the book will be presented in sections dealing with different aspects of the process of coping with kids and in trying to make every moment count. Hopefully, it will be of assistance in this, the most important undertaking of your life.

The general sequence of topics will be about:

1) Focusing on their soul(s) as you parent them.
2) The developmental stage of parenting.
3) The process of parenting in the early formative period.
4) The ages 3 to 7 parenting period.
5) The role requirements of fathering.
6) The role of erotic parameters in parenting.
7) Child care in the coming world.
8) The new soul pools coming in.
9) The problematic parenting patterns dictionary.

PARENT THEIR SOUL!

It is perhaps one of the most inane and insane facts of our life that in the "modern world," kids come last in our priorities. That means that we have taken the anti-Cosmic and anti-biologic stance that tomorrow doesn't matter -- like with global warming. It is essentially a suicidal stance of the paranoid patriarchy that is now dying for reasons just such as this.

The reality is that parenting is the ultimate form of generativity, which is the quintessential form of maturity. It is the building for tomorrow's people and world. In its nature, when we have what we need to do the process, it is a lovely Cosmic and biologic undertaking that unfolds beautiful people. And that is the way it should be. But it isn't the way it's been.

Human formation or the developmental process is an "inverted pyramid" in which the things that happen first (and especially during the intra-uterine period), determine all that happens later. Thus the nine month womb experience and the first three years of life set the pattern for the rest of the individual's experience.

This includes the phenomenon known as "silicone implants" that occur during the "no boundaries" period, especially in the first nine months after birth. These are insertions of the mother's passions and pathological beliefs that operate as though they were the person's own issues until the individual can work them out to the surface to be discharged later in life.

To give an example of how this can work, take a child who is just home from the hospital, say something like 65 hours old. And the parents have read the "scientific" principle that picking up the crying child is conditioning the child to cry.

So they "let the kid cry it out" for 45 minutes, and then they congratulate themselves on the success of their parenting practices -- after all, aren't they all sleeping quietly now, just as predicted?

But now let's look at the person 35 years later via a metaphor here. Suppose we are at the western edge of the Appalachian Mountains and looking west to the eastern edge of the Rocky Mountains. And way over there, we see something.

So we drive for days and finally we arrive at the Grand Canyon. And way down there is the Colorado River -- which in this metaphor is that 45 minutes of ignoring that produced the "inverted pyramid" effect that now makes it all but impossible for the individual to trust intimacy or the Universe.

And this is greatly complicated by the "in loco deity" effect generated by the "commons" child-rearing history of our species for six and a half million years minus ten thousand.

Ten thousand years ago is when the agricultural revolution led us to abandon the practice of the whole village rearing the child on a need requirement basis in the process of having whatever older person in the vicinity meet the needs of the child as they arose.

When the whole community was rearing the child, it was a pretty good cross section of the human race during the period when the child still had one foot planted in the Cosmos, so to speak.

That makes the first three years of the child's experience feel like they are getting the "straight stuff," due to the "hard wiring" arising from our evolutionary process. Early events are then experienced as "God speaking" -- with all the implications, impacts and ramifications that this has.

This is the process that is happening in that first three years -- a phase-down from being a soul out there with full contact with the "Home Office" to a soul being in here and totally immersed in the time/space dimension, the five senses, and all that sort of thing.

What happens during that period affects the individual's relationship to the Cosmos, to the "Home Office" (All That Is), and to themselves as a soul for the rest of their life. And those early experiences really impact, the earlier the more so. This biologic fact profoundly compounds the effects on the individual's emotional body of early negative experiences.

Now going back to our "45 minute kid." A big nick develops in their emotional experiential history around abandonment, rejection by God, and being a person without a Cosmos.

This is the emotional body-based interpretive system in operation. And out of that interpretation comes what John Bradshaw calls the "inner child" in reaction to the "We got trouble right here in River City" in our relationship with the "Home Office" meaning that the child places on that experience.

The result is the formation of a desperate attempt to "get back in the good graces of God," which leads to the pursuit of the "God Housekeeping Seal of Approval" in the form of the individual's trying to bring about a reduction of the negative patterns arising out of the parents' misconceptions and neuroses. In effect, they reached for God and they got "Godzilla," and they then try to please "Godzilla" the rest of their life until they learn better, if ever.

Because of this outcome, the individual is going to have all sorts of reactions and interpretations to all subsequent experiences about who they are, who God is, what their relationship to God is, what their relationship to the human community is, what their expectations and elicitations of treatment from the environment will be, and so on it goes. And out of all this comes the "Grand Canyon."

To make matters more complicated, all human relations and their effects take place at the rate of 16 interactions a second, which is far too fast to control or to be conscious of. And that includes the parenting process of course, and that is where the action is and what the people of tomorrow learn from. Furthermore, it affects the soul via the emotional body, which is the seat of meaning and where all experience lodges.

Meanwhile, this is all taking place in a "double passaging" context. That is, the adults are going through their early adult life phase experiences and the child is unfolding their "developmental ladder" at the same time.

And just to complete to complexity and significance of the thing, the parents are undergoing "developmental recapitulations" as they "back burner remember" what it was like for them at the various developmental stages of their own formative process. And all of this makes for quite an emotionally loaded "stew" in which the person of tomorrow is forming up.

Now, what this means is that everything that happens is going to be affected by all these parameters impacting on the emotional body meaning-making system. Thus, what you are getting is what the child is making of what is happening, rather than just a habit-formation or a socialization process.

For instance, all "consequences" in the "discipline" process are *interpreted* by the individual, and this comes from their soul and from their emotional body. It is these interpretations that they learn, not just some behavior that is modified.

Now if you are doing the parenting process effectively, you are tracking at some level what the forming person's cumulative experiential history has been. This allows you to have some notion of what interpretations they are likely to make of whatever events are happening at the moment.

In other words, you are working with the individual's experience, moment to moment and cumulatively at the back of your mind, so to speak. And at the same time, you are undergoing a major transformation from all this in a 24 hours a day, seven days a week, 365 days a year, 20 year contract process, with all the stakes involved in that.

Meanwhile, all this is taking place with an individual who has a different soul from yours, who has their own intended Destiny, and who is going through the process of forming up while being in your life as you play out your own planned Destiny. And then the whole process takes off with a life of its own.

The requirement here is to have some sort of notion of what the child's cumulative experience has been, what yours has been, and what the relationship between them is -- with particular emphasis on what is happening to the child's soul/emotional body.

One of the prime factors involved here is the so-called "soul age" of the forming individual. "Soul age" is essentially the amount of experience-based soul wisdom the individual has in their soul. This determines both the level of comprehension and the Destiny manifestation of the person-in-the-making.

For instance, younger souls react to things in what could be considered an "immature" manner because they are still learning the "ropes of coping" with being in a physical body in space/time on a "first few times" basis.

This, in turn, means that their Destiny is perforce going to be pretty much a "learning from their mistakes" type of process. Nevertheless, we must still do what we can to make what they learn as cosmically congruent and self-, community- and ecology-committed as possible.

A major consideration of this aspect of the parenting process concerns the degree of congruence between the "soul ages" of the parents and their child(ren). When there is a large distance between the soul ages here, it can be a considerable challenge to deal with.

When, for instance, the child's soul is older than those of the parents, the result is a form of bafflement, befuddlement and bedazzlement in the parents that can really profoundly affect the child-rearing process.

Not infrequently, it will be to one degree or another detrimentally so, due to overwhelm, non-comprehension, fear, envy, exploitation, paranoia or any of a number of other experiences of and reactions from the parents.

And conversely, a much younger soul than the parents precipitates the necessity of allowing the child(ren) to live out their "learning the hard way" Destiny with as little despair, ego-tripping, excessive harm-avoidance, rage, confusion and other "If s/he would only *listen* to me!" reactions from the parents as possible.

The reality is that the fetus/infant/child is a soul who is having reactions to and making interpretations of everything they experience. This requires that you respect their reality, including the fact of the "inverted pyramid effect," the profound helplessness of the infant, the severe handicaps of the child in terms of their knowledge of the workings of the world, their primitive impulse control systems, and the great inner conflicts within the emerging adult during adolescence.

Attempting to be aware as best you can within the complexities of the vicissitudes of life of what is really going on for your child(ren) is the key to effective parenting. And if you play your cards right during the first three year period, the child will shift from being a responsibility to being a resource in many ways, especially if they are an older soul.

It is in essence a cosmic crime to either ignore, assume about or attack children. We have to cover for them as best as we can as they garner their formative experiences, and then to phase ourselves out over time.

Coming from compassionate comprehension of their experience and situation before you put your oar in makes all the difference in the world. It is essential to respect them and their experience.

If you do, they will respect you and your values, and they will then be able to do automatically what you had to do consciously to break the chain of neuroses that has come down for millennia.

Now the way the human system works is that the emotional body is the "seat of meaning." The mental body and the mind/brain acquires, stores, retrieves, processes and presents information, but the emotional body is in effect the bio-computer for the "operator" of the system. Ask any paranoid -- they'll show you how the emotional body determines the meanings of things!

However, the emotional body is also the "seat of the soul" or the "cross-over point" between the soul and the ego, and between the Cosmos and the space/time world. This means that it is fully operative from the very beginning -- from the point of conception onward.

The emotional body therefore does not require a fully functional physical body or brain like the mental body does. This is why people can remember their own conception, intra-uterine experiences and birth process at times.

This means therefore that the emotional body is where the action is. And what that means is that when you are dealing with a fetus/infant/child, you are dealing with a fully conscious soul who is dwelling in the emotional body, while their physical, mental and spiritual bodies are still forming up.

The emotional body is aware of what is happening, regardless of what the mental body or the physical body is capable of comprehending or operating on and manifesting at the time.

This means that experiences impact in two ways -- one at the child's level of conscious mental comprehension and physical capability, and another at the emotional body and soul level. In other words, "the soul knows . . ."

For instance, hypnotic studies have clearly demonstrated that the individual can do things like encode and comprehend exactly foreign language speech by a physician in the next operating room at the point of their birth. Or exactly what took place between their parents at the moment of their conception.

Findings like this prove beyond a reasonable doubt that what is really recording and reacting is the emotional body/soul, with the physical and mental bodies doing a catch-as-catch-can process on the conscious awareness and comprehension capacity level. But everything is going into the emotional body and the person's soul.

What this means then is that the emotional body/soul is tracking, reacting to and interpreting everything far beyond what the biologic/psychological equipment can handle. And that, in turn, means that things like "soul age" (the cumulative soul experience/sophistication of the soul) and "soul types" (the soul's most developed avenues of experience and modes of learning) play a large role in the interpretations that are made by the individual. Thus the soul is what you are actually affecting and dealing with in your parenting. Bottom line.

It is with this in mind that the admonition to respect the child's experience is made. Everything is profoundly affecting both the emotional body and the soul at every step along the way. And the parenting process has to reflect that as much as possible.

The parents being aware of the individual's true nature and experience is absolutely fundamental to the successful formation of a human being. It is this fact that underlies the impact of the awareness training workshops that treat every participant from 6 years old on up as a sentient soul -- and why it works.

Children are people with souls and with an emotional body that is operative from the conception beginning and even before. They need to be treated with the respect and care that this invokes.

Know that everything that is going down around them is going into a sentient soul being whose biologic equipment may not be able to report it, but whose emotional body and soul are being affected forever. At some level, they are getting the whole nine yards of meaning and experience. And the entire crux of the parenting process is the awareness of that fact.

14

Loving commitment, compassionate comprehension, and soul respect will generate an individual who is intensely motivated to be beneficial. It is the nature of the soul, of the species and of the Cosmos to seek to make everything a "win-win proposition."

When the basics are met from the very beginning, the result is an individual who will be seeking to be contributory and compassionate with everything they do. It is the way we are built -- until things like the paranoid patriarchy and our family's neuroses distort us.

In other words, dealing with a fetus/infant/child as a soul, whose emotional body is recording, reacting to and interpreting everything that happens will take you everywhere you want to be in your parenting practice.

GROWING UP WITH THE KID(S)

The parenting process results in a continuously evolving self-image transformation as you go through the various stages of personal development arising from your parenting experiences.

In other words, there are predictable periods with associated experiences, phenomena and consciousness transformations that occur as you go. This brief note is a succinct examination of these stages of parenting.

The first stage is what could be characterized as *"Image Formation."* This covers the period between conception and the birth of the child. What usually happens here is that two fantasies develop about what is going to happen.

One of them is a set of perfectionistic expectations about who the child will be and become, along with what kind of parents you are going to be. And the other is a growing recognition at some level of who this incoming soul is, really.

Out of this set of expectations develops a corresponding set of expectations about how it is going to be with this child. These expectations include images of your role and functioning, the child's personal characteristics and intended Destiny, your pictures of your spouse's family's reactions and pattern, and your ideas about how the community and the Cosmos will respond to your child and to your parenting.

And all of these tend to crystallize into a sort of "pretty picture" of what it will be like. Or, conversely, an image of "hell on wheels" may be forming up in your conscious or sub-conscious mind in reaction to your guesstimates or intuitions about the child and their impact on your life.

The next stage is the *"Attachment"* phase. This covers the period from conception to about 18 months to two years, post-birth. This is the formative period of the operational ego of the child, where their soul and your whole beingness interact to produce whatever core personality is going to come out of the on-going developmental experiences the child has.

The processes involved here are going to both determine and be determined by the degree to which you can attach to another human being at this level of intimacy and required responsibility.

The other big issue that arises in this period is *"Nurturance."* This concerns all the parameters involved in sorting out how much to give to whom, what to give, and how much to expect nurturance yourself. This is a particularly tricky issue in the "isolated nuclear family" situation, where there is such an overload of demands and so little support from the culture.

The third stage is called the *"Authority"* period, and it involves the process of sorting out the reality of your original Images in the light of your child's emerging autonomy and the impact of the widening range of sources of influence on the child(ren).

It becomes a "hot issue" from about age two to age four or five. You are learning about what is a reasonable authority and what is the basis of it, along with having to strike some sort of workable compromise regarding their autonomy and your authority.

The fourth stage runs from about age 3 or 4 years to about 11 or 12 years of age. It is the *"Interpretive"* stage, and it involves figuring out the reality of your concepts of the way things are in life. And of course, a similar process is also going on in your child(ren).

This period covers the "Oedipal/Elektra" process and the so-called "latency age" mid-childhood transition. There is a kind of consolidation and exploratory process going on for the

17

child(ren). In the meantime, you are learning what is realistic to expect out of life arising from all these experiences with your child(ren).

The next stage, the fifth, is the *"Interdependence"* stage, and it covers the period between ages 12 and 18. The children are now going into the transition into adulthood called adolescence, and the "growing away" process commences big time.

It is also a re-run of the *"Authority"* issue, this time with an ever-nearing adulthood separating individual. They are also going through the "I need you and I can't <u>stand</u> that!" process as well. This really puts you through the "They're not yours" and the "They're not you!" factors and lessons of parenting.

Finally, we come to the *"Departure"* stage, where they are or they are *not* leaving "home" to commence their Destiny as an independent individual in the world at large. The impact on you is one of taking stock of your process and results, along with a deep evaluation of yourself as a parent and as a human being. There is also a working out of what kind of relationship you are going to have with your adult child(ren).

This last stage continues more or less through the rest of your life, as the adult life pattern and Destiny of your grown child(ren) plays out and you have whatever form of relationship with them that develops during this stage of the parenting process.

A special aspect of this stage is when the roles start to reverse, so to speak, as you move towards your own departure, while your child(ren) take on the "command generation" position and processes in life.

ON PARENTING

One of the problems with the process of doing parenting is that we all have what could be characterized as biological very intense feelings about it, along with unspoken cultural assumptions about children and about the parenting process. And the reality is that these built-in passions and programmed beliefs are just plain unrealistic.

I was a child clinical psychologist for about 30 years. In all that time, I never did do any teaching or lecturing on parenting per se, because the stuff usually put out about it such as behavioral contingency management and parent effectiveness training just didn't cut it in terms of what is really going on in it and what is needed to do it right.

The difficulty with most of the parenting models and advice that is put out there is that it requires of the people doing the parenting to be some sort of super-human being. If you are going to have to stop and figure out what every single contingency management or parenting intervention that you are going to run on a kid requires or if you are going to have to stop and go into a non-directive therapy enterprise with every incident that comes up with a kid, it just doesn't work.

The truth is that parenting is NOT about concepts or techniques. It is just too damn complicated and profound for that type of thing. My favorite example of this is what I call the "yellow squash incident."

In 1924, John B. Watson, the father of behaviorism, came out with a book on how to do parenting that was touted as the latest scientific findings. It was full of admonitions like don't ever let the child control the situation.

My mother was very impressed with that because of her psychopathology and because of the cultural prestige of science. So when she put yellow squash on my high chair tray when I was nine months old, she promptly put me to bed when I refused to eat it.

When she got me up the next morning, there it was again -- the same piece of yellow squash re-heated. And I spent the morning in my crib. And the afternoon after my "non-lunch." And to bed that night after "dinner." And so it went for three days.

Finally, when it was black and hard from all the re-heating, I threw it at her! But not until I had come to the gut conclusion that she was willing to kill me over a concept and over her mania for control. And the incident became a family legend that proved how incorrigible I was.

Now here we have both a concept and a technique being applied -- with the usual disastrous results of such a process. This doesn't mean that concepts and techniques aren't valid or useful. What it means is that parenting is not about concepts and techniques.

THE NATURE OF PARENTING

Parenting is an *organic generative* process -- building tomorrow's people. It is a "rite of passage" undertaking in which compassionate comprehension and conscientious awareness of what you are generating as experiences and modeling examples of how to function are the intended design of the parenting process.

Also involved in the biologically given design is a respectful and loving commitment to both the present child and to the future adult being able to benefit and to be beneficial. It works on the emotional and mental body development-shaping level, not on the behavior-controlling level.

19

The reality is that children are naturally moral, caring and committed when they come in as an innocent infant. They're just short-sighted, inexperienced, impulsive, lost in the moment, and totally immersed in absorbing all they need to know and to know how to do in order to become a functional human being.

When they do something wrong, they feel terrible about it, and they are trying to figure out what to do about it. And it is our job to help them at such points to achieve the contributory and correct capabilities and outcomes they need and want so badly in the process of living and developing.

Now of course, we all know "monster kids." But that is *not* usually born in, though such "bad seed" kids do show up sometimes. What they represent is some sort of genetic aberration, a primitive consciousness soul, and/or a destiny design for this life with the intent of working something through on the Cosmic level in this lifetime.

The cause of almost all cases of truly negative manifestation from a child from the git-go is *damaged goods.* That is, the family circumstances and the parenting processes are so distorted and destructive that they produce irreparable damage to the ego of the child.

By the way, such situations are part of the destiny design by the soul in which it is deemed essential that the soul expand their beingness through the "school of hard knocks" for this lifetime.

That having been said, the characterization of the innocent infant described above is the fundamental truth about human nature and about who children really are. The fact that we so seldom see the innocent infant is that life has been very harsh throughout human history as we climbed the ladder of learning the ropes of how to handle time/space reality.

THE HISTORY OF PARENTING

In the past, we operated out of a very different conception of parenting. Childhood wasn't recognized as a separate period and process of development until the middle ages, and adolescence wasn't acknowledged until society became too complex to enter at the onset of puberty, due to the industrial order's appearance on the scene.

And throughout all that until the latter half of the last century, children and teenagers were regarded as "criminal personalities" -- as miniature adults who were acting in a highly selfish, short-sighted and seditious manner.

It was recommended that you start beating them into conformity at six months of age via "proper caning" as the disciplinary/teaching process. The idea was that if we didn't do that, they would enter adulthood as utter "moral cretins."

Up till now, society all over the world has basically been going through the process I call the "school of hard knocks" with "evil" as the "headmaster" for some six and a half million years.

Now "evil" is "live" spelled backwards. It means learning from your mistakes, violating the Laws of the Cosmos in the process, for which you pay the Karma and the consequences. It takes no imagination to know what *that* produced. History speaks for itself.

But this also led to our learning a lot from that process along the way to where we are now. However, it precipitated a lot of paranoia and negative assumption, with the resulting conceptions of everything, including the nature of children and how we should rear them.

The parenting process has been basically done in that context. So what you get is a lot of the parenting process that has been composed of two things. One of them is this kind of primitive consciousness sort of process, some of which is biologically driven and some of it lack of soul sophistication caused.

The other part of it is a process that could be described as a distortion of what is the natural process that we evolved with in the first place. What happened originally in our evolution was that when we did the shift over from primate to hominoid to human, we were originally a kind of a troop of organisms that effectively ate out the area we were in over time. And then we would move on.

We had this kind of moving territory thing that would take about a year to carry off. And we did a rotating migration thing so that in about a year we would be back where we started, and everything would have replenished itself. It was a sort of ecologically balanced process.

The way that worked was that each individual or little cluster that we would call a 'family' would have a little nitch somewhere in the area in which they were eating and living. And there would be a large central area in which everybody was in constant contact and interaction.

This "commons system" as it is called, where there is a large central area in which there is a lot of contact between people resulted in a natural support happening all over the place.

And of course, there would also be natural conflicts occurring here and there as well. But by and large, there was a lot of what you could characterized as mutual contact and support that went on in the commons area.

This generated the thing called the "in loco parentis," where whoever was a non-child would take care of what the child needed on a requirement-meeting basis. In effect, everybody reared all the children as if they were the parents.

What that effectively meant was that the whole troop was involved in the child-rearing process. Every adolescent and adult would basically pass on lessons and administer needed discipline, nurture and support.

Now what this did with regard to the biologic parenting process was to take it past the shortcomings of the biological parents that we all have as human beings, and the parents' neuroses got diffused into the whole community contact process.

Now of course a certain number of the members of the community would be the occasional hard ass or psychotic, dullard or cold case that would do damaging things to the kids.

But they were one or two of the 250 or so individuals involved in the child-rearing process, and their occasional scaring and scarring wouldn't leave what you would characterize as permanent damage in the children.

In the meantime, the kid imprinted on virtually every type of person in the human community because they would in fact over time have some sort of bonding connection with everybody.

To a lesser extent, the same sort of thing happened with regard to the business of the other social needs. For instance, those of the parents. So there was in effect a constant nexus of people who would be there as support people for the parents.

So that when the family unit returned to their little nitch area, they would have all had a day of social contact with various members of the community. And they would bring that social enrichment to each other in a kind of "cup runneth over" manner. And they would also interact with each other in an actual personal relationship kind of way.

This "hunter-gatherer" pattern continued until about ten thousand years ago when the agricultural revolution took place. What we did with the agricultural thing was that we decided to put down roots in a given area and we would cultivate the plants that we were going to eat. And then we domesticated some animals that we were also going to eat or that we were going to consume the products from. This all radically altered the system out of which we lived.

Now this change did generate advances that created for us benefits that led to increased longevity, quality of life and other things that are undeniable. But there were also great costs that are undeniable as well.

What happened is that the requirements of cultivation and domestication led to each "family" to have a rather large plot of land which they lived on and care-took as they raised the food they needed.

And people lived in domiciles scattered around a large central area to which they would come for exchange and contact. But not every day because there was so much maintenance that had to be done in their private domiciles and farmlands.

With regard to the parenting process, we have the shift of the responsibility of that process from the whole community to the following situation. Over here, we have the farm house. In that farmhouse is the mother, the older female children, the younger children and the elders.

And then out there somewhere in this surrounding plot of land are the father and the older male children, and they are out there working the fields, herding the animals, and such. And then we go across the sizeable territory of the family land and we come to the border of the next farm. And we cross that land area to the next farmhouse.

As you can tell immediately, we are sitting here with a very different situation with regard to how the parenting responsibilities and processes go. Now there is still the partial extended family in the farmhouse, but there is a gigantic reduction in the amount of support and the variety of people involved in the process of the child-rearing, and the males have in effect been removed from both parenting and social contact.

Now of course over time things like the quilting bee and the church social and the barn-raising occurred that provided a partial return to some of the missing social support that had been there before. But we never really recovered from the loss of the commons, so to speak.

THE DEVELOPMENTAL PROCESS

Kids are extremely active and searching, learning organisms that are seeking to acquire an entire culture in the first three years of life. In Switzerland, for instance, it is quite common for children by the age of three to know how to speak five languages -- Swiss, German, Italian, French and English.

They pick them up as if it was nothing because all five languages are spoken all around them all the time. The other reason is that kids are extremely active and absorptive during the first three years of life.

In fact there is a biologic term that very specifically and technically refers to the kind of thing that is involved in this process. It is called "imprinting," and Lawrence Tinbergen discovered it. He found that if you run a shoe box ahead of a group of goslings, they will fall into line behind it, and they regard it as their mother due to its size and rate of movement.

Unlike ducklings and goslings, though, kids don't have a three hour span in which any stimulus smaller than an elephant will do the job. It is not that simple for us. But for the first three years, their experiences do have a kind of broad imprinting effect. These early experiences become the foundation for the entire personality and life career that the person manifests.

Now for us, because of the ensoulment process, we are souls wearing a space/time vehicle, so to speak. We were out there in the Cosmos until we came into our vehicle in here. And consequently, we had a very actively involved relationship with the "Home Office" out there.

And so when we come in as a soul and we enter the body, we then hit this biological highly intensive searching and absorbing process of early childhood experience, and we end up effectively going into what I call the "in loco Deity" phenomenon.

What I mean by that is that the soul comes together with the intense seeking thing, and there is this vague remembrance of what just was out there that ties in with the enormously powerful imprinting period of the first three years where you acquire the entire culture.

This creates the desperate desire to re-unite with the "Home Office," and we reach out for God and we get "Godzilla," in the form of non-acceptance all the way out to out and out rejection from our mother, and we start the frantic effort to "earn the God Housekeeping Seal of Approval" from this God-stand-in, as we try to close the gap between us and her.

This then gets merged with the absorption of the entire culture in the first three years of life, and we get "hooked on the most rejecting parent" and on "desperately seeking Susan" in the form of acceptance from the culture as well as from first our mother and then from stand-ins for the original cast people.

As a result of all this, the kid acquires both a personality based on seeking to terminate the so-called rejection by God and the absorption of the fundamentals of the entire culture they find themselves in.

Until fairly recently, the entire culture was no more complex than that of a small village. And so a seven year old could negotiate an adult role in that kind of culture. This is where the Catholic Church got the concept of the "age of reason" at age seven. It also coincides with a physiologic brain change at that time.

In the middle ages, it was not uncommon to see seven year olds done up in the full court regalia or in the full costume of the working peasant adult. This is why childhood was not recognized as a very different psychology of beingness at that time.

This resulted in the business of phasing off the Cosmos out there and the becoming fixated on life here as the be-all-to-end-all of our existence. And the kid basically transferred the face of God onto their imprinting parent figures in the "in loco Deity" thing.

The functional biological purpose of this whole phenomenon is to get the kid to acquire the entire culture and their basic personality by age three. And you have to take the culture as "God's Gospel Truth" or you are not going to acquire your ego operating system in time.

So the first three years are a period of biologic imprinting of the extremely active learning process of the child in conjunction with a phase-down of their relationship with the "Home Office."

As a function of all that, the "Home Office" gets transferred to the parents or to whoever is doing the child caring. Now when they were doing that in the commons, they transferred their relationship with the "Home Office" to the entire community, and the whole process had the effect of sort of filling in and doing rather well in that transitional process.

RETURNING TO OUR PARENTING HISTORY

But with the onset of the agricultural revolution, we hit the "isolated nuclear family" situation, and the relationship to the Cosmos all transfers down to one person, usually the mother because the father is out of the home most of the time. And that meant that one person was now required to do what the whole village used to do.

Furthermore, this meant that if you were male, you were supposed to keep your personal feelings, experiences and needs to yourself, you were the "buck stops here" person and you were a technical resource for the culture. They were trained to be unemotional, non-relational, and non-comprehending of the deeper qualities of human manifestation and existence, and the paranoid patriarchy was born.

The shift from the commons to the isolated nuclear family as the child-rearing agent was now complete. There is nothing wrong with the nuclear family. That is a biological necessity and the profoundest relationship other than the spousal relationship that you will ever encounter.

The problem is the isolation of the nuclear family. We are in a situation where we are asked to do single-handedly what the entire community used to do. And that is the true reality of the parenting process in the modern world.

So we then went from the agricultural to the industrial/urban environment, and that made the situation even worse. And this was especially true after the turn of the twentieth century, when we added the *impersonal* urban environment to the stew.

23

There was a time when the neighborhood functioned like a mini-commons. Everyone was involved with everybody. But since we have gone impersonal, the child-rearing situation has gotten to what could be characterized as a biologic nightmare.

It is basically not possible to do the child-rearing process successfully under these conditions. In other words, you end up starting out with the parenting thing in a guaranteed failure of the whole undertaking situation.

It is simply not going to work, in the sense of your being able to meet your own needs and those of your spouse and the needs of your kids and the requirements of the community all at once and all by yourself. It is simply impossible to pull off.

What we have now is a "super-selfishness" in the way we do everything, and commons type living just can't work at all under these circumstances. If we try it, we end up in the "L.C.D." type of situation.

What that means is that the individuals in the group who are the most antisocial and aggressive or passive-aggressive dominate the whole culture. Then the co-dependent rescuers try to compensate for what these individuals are doing. And they end up burning themselves out, and eventually the whole thing deteriorates to the level of the level of the most selfish and damaging in the group. That is the "lowest common denominator" outcome as we try to complexly compromise in an attempt to minimize the amount of damage done to everybody by this effectively totally unworkable situation, and we end up with everything reducing to the most primitive and negative processes and outcomes.

The reason for all this is that the collective consciousness is still doing the "What's in it for me?" as opposed to the "What's in it for We?" process of living. "What's in it for me?" is a win/lose proposition in which what I gain is going to be at your expense. And what you gain is going to result in insufficient resources to go around.

The only way out of this is to return to the commons way of living and child-rearing. We have to return to the "generative society," where we can entrust our children and ourselves to each other, and where we can have it work effectively.

In order to do that, we have to do a complete reversal of our values and priorities in the culture at large and in the child-rearing process. Right now we are running off the "Big P's" -- Power, Paranoia, Patriarchy, Prerogative, Pride, Privilege, Perks, Prestige and so on, along with the "Big R's" -- Rage, Revenge, Racism, Rape and the like. We have no choice but to shift to the "Big C's" -- Commitment, Compassion, Caring, Connection, Concern, Contribution, Co-creation, Competence, Community, and so on.

And that is essentially where we are headed. And after we have made the transition transformation of consciousness that is in the process of going down now, we will be able to start setting up what could be characterized as the reinstatement of the various forms of the commons arrangement so we can start getting biologically sane again. And at that point, we will not have nearly as much difficulty with the parenting process.

It is a testimony and a major tribute to the incredible resilience and commitment of the collective consciousness of the human race that we have done as well as we have, given the conditions we have been laboring under for hundreds of thousands of years.

It is amazing considering the vulnerability of children and the enormous cost and overwhelm of the parenting process of the isolated nuclear family that we are in fact as well put together as we are at this time. It is a tribute to the human spirit.

THE SEVEN GENERATION PROCESS

Now another aspect of the whole rather astounding history of the human race that we have had to deal with is reflected in a statement from the Bible that goes something like, "And the sins of the fathers shall be passed on to the sons for seven generations."

First of all, notice the Calvinistic, chauvinistic and patriarchal wording of that quote. What would probably be a better way of putting it is "The mistakes of the parents shall be passed on to the children for seven generations."

Now the seven generations thing is another one of those "nature's biologic ways" of handling the realities of the fact that we are technically known as "plastic" beings. What that means is that we are not instinct-driven. We are learning machines.

To see the difference, let's take the ants as an example. They develop very complex social structures with all kinds of elaborate divisions of labor. Take the army ants. They eat everything in their path by having a division of labor so that various and sundry ants of different designs are in various places in the marching column so the thing works perfectly.

Now you would think that this is a very complex and sophisticated system. But when you watch what actually happens, you see what is really going on. What takes place is that at the end of the day, one of the ants -- the lead ant of the column -- goes up a tree and it proceeds to attach its claws around the branch, and it hangs upside down.

And then the next ant in the column hangs onto him or her. And pretty soon, the whole colony is one gigantic sort of tear drop-shaped red thing. That is how they spend the night sleeping.

Then the next morning, the first rays of the sun hit the outer layer of the ants. That activates them, and they loosen their grip, with the result that they fall to the ground. And that exposes the next layer of ants, and they fall to the ground. And so on and so on and so on.

And what happens is that because of the physical shapes of the various kinds of ants, as they hit the ground or the pile of ants, and they fall into place in the developing column by the shape of who each ant is. Then the lead ant takes its first move and it leaves a chemical trail behind it.

And the other ants follow that trail completely blindly. And voila! A complex multi-functional division of labor of sub-columns makes up the unstoppable machine on the march, eating its way along.

When I was a kid, it was not uncommon to find what you would characterize as a spiral ant graveyard on the sidewalk. What would happen there is some rageful little boy would poke the lead ant into a spiral marching path. Then all the other ants would march behind it to their deaths in a spiral pattern because they are mechanically and chemically run.

Now that is the other end from being "plastic." That means that the ants' societal structure is strictly done by pure mechanics and chemistry. We, on the other hand, have almost no such built-in automatic pilot hard-wired structures and behaviors.

There are some subtle social/interactive and ecologically guided instinct-like patterns around things like the sexual stuff and the care-taking of the young. That is about all that is left in us that is partly instinct-driven. And even that is highly "plastic" in its manifestation. And there are zero purely mechanical or chemical systems beyond basic physiological functions, and even those are highly subtly and complexly multi-determined and even affected by mental, emotional and Cosmic forces and decision processes at some level.

That means therefore that we basically do things by learning rather than by hard wiring. And in a very real way, that means that each individual with their unique learning history of experiences becomes a highly unpredictable system that is different from every other individual.

Now a relatively hidden implication of that situation is that if you had *complete* learning domination, the result would be chaos. The whole system would disintegrate very quickly.

So nature's way of handling the problem that as highly complex, sophisticated and ensouled beings we need to have *both* adaptability and stability is to set up this "seven generation" thing.

What that means is that for seven generations back, you have what could be described as a quasi-imprinting during the first three years of life. As a result of it, you end up following the learning's of the preceding six generations. That provides seven generations of stability of how we do things.

Then in the eight generation, everyone has to innovate on all the areas that were imprinted for seven generations because that seven generation back ecology has by now changed enough to become irrelevant.

And the seventh generations -- the trainers of the eighth generation -- pass along their *learned* experiences in this life to their child(ren). What you therefore have is a seven generation span of stability that allows for the continuity of culture.

And simultaneously, the individual learning process allows for the adaptability to the ever-changing circumstances of their lives. This allows for continuous adaptation and modification of how we operate in response to new circumstances to be built in and passed on.

This combination thereby provides both for predictability and adaptability in a family culture pass-on mechanism that is *not* passed on via DNA/genetics. By using the "This is the way we do things" (until things change) cultural transmission process, we are highly flexible and responsive while still being stable and predictable enough to allow order to be there as well.

This family culture pass-on effect is rather misleading from the outside looking in, because it looks like there is genetic code transmission going on here. But it is actually family *culture* transmission.

So that is why nature did it that way. But it has had the effect in the isolated nuclear family of passing on the family neuroses for seven generations. So then you get this seven generation back process and all that going on along with the "in loco Deity" phenomenon for the individual to handle at the same time.

So we've got quite an insane situation going on, all things considered. And again, let me remind you of the remarkableness of our survival and of the degree to which we have managed keep the human species going under these biologically seemingly impossible conditions. We are indeed a startlingly resilient species.

All of this is why this section of the presentation is talking about the nature of how the parenting process got so heavy. It is because of all the resultants of the isolated nuclear family situation.

Now what that means is that what you get is a whole set of rather difficult conditions that hold in the parenting process. For instance, the parenting relationship is largely a "one way street" thing in which the energy goes from the parent to the child.

This is because the children are a learning system and they are also the investment of the whole species in its future. And of course, there is also the whole thing of the biologic process called the "selfish gene." The general notion here is that the genes use the organism as their "carrier" with the intention of replicating themselves, regardless of the cost to the individual person.

The title of this phenomenon is a good description of the genetic process, and it is also a demonstration of both the biologic domination of our operation and of the selfishness of the soul consciousness we have been manifesting up to this time.

We have been climbing the ladder of the first three chakras of soul consciousness in our history as the human soul collective mastered the challenges of time/space on this planet. The first chakra has to do with the lessons of physical survival, the second with those of emotional survival, and the third with those of social and ecological survival.

At this point, the high point of the bell-shaped curve of the collective consciousness of the whole species is at the top of the third chakra. We are in effect poised to enter the fourth chakra as a soul collective.

Though that means that half the human race knows better than to be selfish at this time, it is the lower half of the curve, the ones who don't know any better than being selfish, that are the ones that run the show right now because that has had to be the process by which the human race has evolved.

So that means that those who are basically primitive and willing to use coercion, corrosion and corruption as their process of doing things are the ones with all the guns, money and power right now.

Meanwhile, those who know better are the ones who have to somehow get their values, modus operandi and wisdom in around the cracks when nobody is looking. This is essentially what has been going on for some time.

THE NEXT DEVELOPMENT

And this is, of course, the end of that phase of the collective consciousness evolution of the human race. We've been there, done that, and wrung that rag dry, thank you. The present era is either the end of the human race or the end of selfishness in the human race, one or the other. It is as plain and simple as that.

The present era is the long predicted "Armageddon" in which the human race stands at the "Y" in the road point choosing which way it is going to go -- up or out. The message of Armageddon is that "Selfishness is suicide. Period. End of report. On the individual and the collective level." So we are seeing the end of all that, though not without an implosion of the system and quite a resistance on the part of the lower half of the consciousness curve.

And of course, there will be a massive change in the way everything works in the future as a function of the fact that if we get past this growth crisis, our value and consciousness base will move into the Cosmic manifestation process right here in time/space.

We are truly "on the threshold of a dream" as we basically commit to the next step in the evolution of human consciousness, which is *coming from the heart.* It is the next logical and no-choice natural step.

The problem is that after six and a half million years of a totally terrorizing history, we are really scared to do it. And so therefore we have to go through the tearing down of the paranoid patriarchy that is preventing us from going up.

We also have to undergo the exodus of the primitive and pathological paranoid souls who would continue to prevent us from doing so. Meanwhile we have the simultaneous emergence of a huge number of souls who can pull this off like Lincoln did in the shepherding in of the industrial order.

These times are actually playing out exactly as was predicted. It is a "Cosmic kick in the butt." We have to get over our fear and to get into love as the only way to fly. And have been building to this point for all of our history. We now have to get it together or get out.

So the process that is going down at this point will result in a total transformation of the collective consciousness of the human race, and the pattern of evil-domination on the mass level that has been the warp and woof of the human race will come to an end.

Evil as a choice option for individuals will, of course, continue, but it will not be the mass consciousness any more. And so we are going through a gigantic change of everything at this time. And one component of it will, of course, be the drastic transformation of the circumstances of the parenting process.

THE CHALLENGES OF PARENTING

For now, though, we need to focus on what the parenting process has meant to us under the conditions of the past, so that we get some notion of (a) what happened to us, (b) what happens when we tried to parent, (c) why kids are blasting their parents' heads off for what they did to them, and all that kind of stuff.

For instance, there was an anthropologist by the name of Jules Henry who did a very unusual thing, which was to study his own culture. He did things like go into the elementary and high schools, the advertising industry, and even into the homes of emotionally disturbed children. He learned and shared a tremendous amount about how our culture works.

For instance, he learned that the primary lesson taught in public schools is never to lose control or to lose in competition, and to hate the winner. So you get this process of always trying to control everything and always scrambling for the top and being hated for being either a loser *or* a winner.

That pattern gets passed on to or gets involved in the process of working with our children as we rear them. This happens because the kids have to learn how to be effective competitors and control-deflectors in the world at large as its been.

And simultaneously, we have to be able to survive with the kids, and we also have to deal with our own competitive and control patterns ourselves as a function of what *we* went through.

So then you get into what you could call a "squabbling siblings" kind of model of what the child-rearing process ends up looking like between you and your kids. Because what typically happens in a lot of this kind of stuff is that when you have an adult who is overwhelmed to the max, that the adult deteriorates or gets devolved into their own inner child. So you have a five year old kid trying to rear a seven year old kid.

And the control and competition thing really gets into quite a complicated process with regard to the child-rearing thing. And what do you think the kids are learning from all this?

This control/competition thing is derived from one of the two common underlying assumptions about who children are as a kind of generally assumed model of how they work.

Up to the industrial revolution, you didn't have "children," you had "little ones." And then you had farm hands or saleable labor or extra help around the house and that kind of thing. And then they left the family early.

The concept of adolescence didn't kick in until the First World War, when we began have more and more complicated white collar or verbally mediated work. There therefore was the necessity for a longer period of learning and enculturation before an individual could participate in the world of work. So schooling was extended.

And from these relatively recent origins came the various assumptions about who children are. And the two big ones were "children as unsocialized monsters" and "children as innocent cherubs."

The "children as unsocialized monsters" means the whole business of control and competition battles, and you had better damn well control a kid or it will control you. That's where the concept of "spare the rod and spoil the child" came from.

Just a piece of information about how extreme this stuff got, there was a guy named Schreiber who was regarded as *the* expert pediatrician. He wrote a book about how to raise children. It was the Dr. Spock book from 1860 to 1960, when it was still being published.

The book was a prescription for torture, and there were many torture devices he gave detailed information on how to construct and utilize. I can only remember one. What it was, was a little wrap-around leather strap thing at the base of the back and another one at in mid-back, with a vertical leather strap in between.

The lower and middle back straps were horizontal and wrapped around the child's body. There was another vertical strap up on the front of their body. There was also this wooden stick that comes up from the lower strap sticking out from the chest at a slight angle. And at the end of the stick was the working end of a nail at about chin level.

It was strapped to the child in the classroom where the Professor held forth for long hours. And when the child fell asleep, their head would come down and the working end of the nail would pierce their chin.

So what you have here is a situation where there is the "child as monster" model, and you had to control them completely or they would run amok and control you and devastate everything.

The other end of the mythology around children was the "child as cherub." That means that the child is extremely vulnerable, like a delicate egg shell, and that you have to be very careful lest you crush it.

And you must be equally careful that it not harm itself, which meant that it had to be continuously supervised and hands-on handled in order to avoid their getting into harm's way. If you have ever heard an adult shriek, "My God, you'll KILL yourself!" when they see a child climbing a tree, you have seen this dynamic in action.

Of course, one of the things that paradoxically happens is that if you say that often enough is that you will have built in a program to harm themselves and to be afraid of harm at all times. The kid picks up the parent's constant concern that they are going to kill themselves.

Now human interaction takes place at the rate of 16 exchanges a second, which is beyond our consciousness and control. It is run by the emotional body, and it is therefore determined by our true feelings, many of which are unconscious.

And children tune in to that sixteenth of a second messaging very intensely, with profound resultants. And if you constantly fear their harm, they will come to believe that they are going to harm themselves.

And then there is another rather ironic outcome of this excessive harm-avoidance approach. And that is that the child may end up doing a "bending over backwards" tack or an "I'll show THEM!" attitude, with the result that they engage in hair-whitening high risk-taking at an alarming rate.

So what we have is a new set of expectations and processes around these emerging developmental role expectations of young people. And it is taking place in the context of the isolated nuclear family situation.

Now there are all kinds of things involved in this isolated nuclear family process. One of these is the "guaranteed failure" situation. We simply can't reproduce the resources of the entire community single-handed as we raise our kids. And you can't beat yourself up because you can't.

On top of which, we come down here to time/space to go through the business of taking on the extreme density of this dimension. We are beings that have a soul inside a physical vehicle.

We therefore have the capacity to exercise free will and therefore to greatly expand our experience. But at the same time, you have to do that in the context of everyone else's free will and in the context of the toughness and density of third dimension space/time.

What that effectively means is that the process of living life consists of going up to the plate, and you basically try to take a crack at making a hit come out of that. And life is about batting averages, rather than about success as a result.

It's about sometimes you win, sometimes you lose, but always you keep on going. And the idea is to keep your batting average as high as possible, but you don't harass yourself if you aren't hitting a thousand. That is literally impossible, and you can't expect to hit a thousand, period.

Now professional athletes have spent a major part of their lives developing themselves to the point where they are at the peak of their capacity and at the peak of their performance in competition with the best in the biz in every way.

Under these kinds of conditions, a batting average of .300, or 30%, is pretty damn good. So an effective way of looking at the process of rearing children is that if you are going for batting .300, and if you make it, you are doing pretty damn well.

It is just such a heavy situation that the best model for looking at how you go about the process of rearing kids is to expect to try for .300, not a thousand. If you don't know that that is the best you can expect, you can get into some pretty deep self-disgust over that. And that ultimately translates into child-hatred, a state of deep demoralization, and so on.

So one of the things that are helpful for you to do when you are carrying out the child-rearing process is to have the expectation of hitting around .300, given the circumstances you are working under. Remember the resilience of the human race, and remember the fact that there is a soul inside that kid, and that they have more equipment that you might possibly think.

Like one of my favorite examples about this kind of thing is the back of a hand that sends the kid careening across the room and up against the wall. That is definitely not a positive event.

But when the kid has been driving you up the wall with a screaming temper tantrum and with constant bugging and negative behavior for the last three hours and you have given them six warnings about your being ready to explode, and *then* you let fly with the hand, they can understand it.

What throws kids is when they get the back of the hand on a "Jekyll-Hyde" chaotic, unpredictable and undeservedly unnecessary basis. That kind of thing *does* do serious harm and is to be avoided like the plague.

That doesn't mean that I am condoning or advocating violence towards kids here. I know that every experience goes down deep in there with them. It's just that things have to *make fair sense* to them.

I remember once one my kids gave me holy hell when she was an adult about an experience that happened to her when she was about eight. Her mother was a rather ferocious person against whom I had no real defenses.

She was very firm about the fact that while we were at a drive-in movie, the kids were damn well going to be in their "nuggies," you know with the foot coverings and the zipper up the front. We had the back seat all rigged up as a bed for them.

That was our graduate school form of family entertainment. For five bucks, we would get a double feature, etc. at the drive-in. But she insisted that it was too much fuss and feathers to bring the kids home fully dressed, and then to have to change them before bedding them down. I thought that was a little rigid but tolerable.

Well I found out from my daughter that they had never gotten over the horrible humiliation weekend after weekend of having to walk back to the rest room in their nuggies when everyone else was dressed in normal street clothes.

You see kids record and remember everything. Those things go down and they go down deep. And the "inverted pyramid" phenomenon of early experiences shaping all subsequent learning is a very real reality.

Like with the crying themselves to sleep thing that I described earlier. For the kid, this is 15 or 45 minutes on the first day at home. That's 15 to 45 minutes out of say two days of their life by that time.

How long do you think fifteen minutes of crying feels like to a kid? To them, every instant is an eternity. For them, it feels like this is going to be what it is like forever. And that burns in like a wood-burning wand. So what the kid does is to start to react to that. And their reaction starts to affect the environment's reaction, and you get a self-fulfilling prophesy effect that starts building.

Like for instance, one of the things that they found out in the infantology field is that kids who are receiving too many of these kinds of experiences engage in a response called "back-arching."

Normally an infant who feels comfortable with the universe will mold immediately, and they will try to get their head as near the heart beat in the adult's chest to get the thump, thump, thump that was there throughout their intra-uterine experience.

But a kid who has had too much of the "let them cry it out" experience will react to being picked up with back-arching. This of course feels to the person picking them up like they suddenly are holding this bent board.

The message they get from the kid is, "Put me *down!*" And the adult is feeling something like, "Oh my God! Sorry!" and they hastily put the kid back down. As you can see, you get a self-fulfilling prophesy effect going here.

So then you look at this person who is now 35 years old. The top of the inverted pyramid looks to us something like the Midwest of the United States, which was once an ocean floor.

So it looks like miles and miles of nothing but miles and miles -- like a big flat surface. And way over there you see something that you drive over to, and you get to the lip of the Grand Canyon.

And down there at the base of the Canyon is the Colorado River where it all got started. The individual is now an "urban hermit" who has very little capacity to let love in or to be in any way vulnerable and available to emotional closeness. So, little things mean a lot, especially early on.

This kind of thing is a part of the "guaranteed failure" factor in parenting, given the isolated nuclear family thing and the nature of our culture now. As was said earlier, kids come last in our value priorities. And that is very intense in its implications and ramifications.

And again, it is a tribute to our survival capacity, to our resilience, to our ingenuity, and to our determination to make a win out of this thing no matter what that we are still here. It is this that has made it possible to pull off hanging in there. This is where the batting .300 comes in. We have the right stuff to keep on truckin.'

Another component of this whole process of working with kids is the thing I call the "urge to kill." This is the mother handing the child to the father saying, "Take her before I kill her!"

This arises because of the circumstances we are talking about in the isolated nuclear family, which are such a continuous assault on the sensibilities and the resources of the adult that it is inevitable that some such intensely frustrating rage will eventually show up, from time to time at least.

And with most of us carrying the neuroses of seven generations before us, it not infrequently comes up. Then we get all freaked out about that -- "What kind of a human being am I? What kind of parent am I that I would want to strangle my kid!?"

In the first place, the reality about the whole process is that one of nature's funny compromises is that we had to forage for long distances for food at one point in our evolutionary history. The sun novad for about ten thousand years.

That dried up the jungle and put us into a veldt environment, thereby taking away the leaves and the food. That is when became omnivorous because there just wasn't enough edible vegetation around.

The other thing that happened at the same time was that we had to survive on the ground without the kind of protection the trees had provided. We ended up "tender morsels on the hoof."

We're not big, we are not fast, we don't have fangs, we don't have claws, we don't have horns, we don't have shells, we don't have poison, we don't have a stinger, and we don't have camouflage. We were sitting ducks for the nearest saber tooth tiger.

What we *did* have was a primitive form of vocal and nonverbal communication, which allowed us to share information. So that if I see something that you don't and I let you know that, everybody in the area then knows that and all survived.

Like if I go, "Ho-o-o-o!!!," that means you better beat feet and get the hell out of there as there is a saber tooth back there. And we all take off in different directions, leaving the tiger confused.

This greatly increased our brain size, which increased the skull size. Meanwhile, the chimpanzee's pelvis is a little flimsy cartilage structure because all it is, is a hinge for moving the leg muscles.

So when the food supply dried up and we had to forage for long distances, we had to go upright for the longer strides and the ergonomic efficiency. It took too much energy to go on all fours. But that put two thirds of the body weight on the pelvis. This quickly led to the huge bone that it became. And as a strength-builder, the hole in the center got smaller.

Now we've got a little problem here. Our head is bigger and the hole is smaller. And so what nature did to handle this was to effectively drop the kid out of the womb half way through gestation. Zoologically speaking we should carry our young in the womb for 18 months.

So that means that therefore the kid comes out notoriously helpless. No other new born child of any species is as helpless as ours is. So nature had to fast come up with some way to extend the protection of the uterus to outside.

Nature used a couple of techniques. One of them was a thing called the "cute" response. Anything with a big face, round cheeks, large eyes and certain movement patterns will elicit the *"A-a-aw!"* response. And we want to pick it up, care for it, nurture it and play with it and all that sort of stuff. In effect nature extended the intra-uterine environment by making everybody instinctively respond to the "cute" quality of the baby.

The other strategy nature used is that the single most grating sound in the world to us is that of a screaming child. We will do almost anything to terminate that gawd awful sound. Talk to any battering parent and they'll tell you, "I *HAD* to make that noise stop!"

That guaranteed that we would pick up the kid when they were in distress as part of the extension of the intra-uterine environment. But the aversiveness of that noise goes with us throughout our lives, so that a crying child will drive a parent up the wall very quickly.

Hence, the "urge to kill." Especially after the 17th time that they have spilled a glass of milk, they are throwing a temper, they refuse to stop any of it, you can't find their god-damned shoes, and all that stuff in an endless series of frustrations with the kid has been happening.

And since there is nobody else to take over when the urge comes, you get this thing of having to sit on it, to shove it down, to pretend it doesn't exist. And then you have the whole question of "What kind of a human being am I that I would be that angry at my kid?" The answer is "a perfectly normal one." It is part of the process of rearing kids.

But most of us have been taught by our rather bizarre culture that we must never, ever be angry at our children. And that, of course, is basically very bad pedagogy for parents. It just doesn't make any sense and it is fundamentally unreal. Especially in the light of our priorities and our putting of kids (and parents) needs last.

Kids are very difficult to deal with, period. Especially in the isolated nuclear family in which one person has to do it all under intensely deprived and infuriating circumstances. We obviously need to completely re-arrange our priorities and our pragmatics.

Then there is the fact that child-rearing is the toughest job in the world -- just ask any day care worker or teacher. Even under conditions of the commons, it is the toughest and yet the most important job there is.

It is after all the building of the people of tomorrow and of the next seven generations. And if you think about the cost, complexity, difficulty and processes involved in building a Department of Philosophy, or in putting together an automobile, and then you think about the complexity and commitment involved in putting a human being together, you get some idea of what I mean by the "toughest job in the world."

The one who is doing the child-rearing in the isolated nuclear family is overwhelmed and strung out a lot of the time. It is an incredibly high stakes, tremendously demanding, very poorly understood, and really badly supplied and supported occupation in our society and in almost all world cultures at the present time.

All of this needs to be taken into account in your .300 batting average thing. It is terribly important to be fair with yourself and to be easy on the kid around these kinds of considerations, because it is just the reality of the situation.

But most of us are never told about these kinds of things, or if we are told of them, we are told them by our own angry parents who are informing us that we are the world's worst problem and the cause of all their problems. And then we end up as the "guilt bank of the world" out of the "guilt-wilt" reaction. Or we hear it from people who are just generally hostile, and we discount what they are saying.

It is essential that we start educating people about this kind of stuff in school in the process of preparing them for life. They need to know what is really involved, both for the preparing them for the job at hand and so that they don't get involved in all sorts of freak-outs about what they encounter when they actually do things without any training.

About the only thing most of us have when we entering parenting is what we experienced at the hands of our parents. Or you get those irrelevant recommendations about don't condition crying or sitting down and doing therapy with the kid over everything.

BOUNDARY ISSUES

Another component of this whole parenting process is boundary issues. Especially during the first nine months after birth, in which there are no boundaries between the parent and the kid, and the kid is all needs, with little self-directed behavior or ability to tell the self from the world.

Now remember, the period from birth to nine months should be the latter half of the intra-uterine experience, given our zoology. As another component of the uterus-extending compromise that nature used, is this what is known as the "symbiotic" period.

It means that the mother and the child during this time are biologically linked and completely bonded, regardless of gender and everything else. They are a "double bubble" with each other.

Because of the biology and because of the isolation of the nuclear family, the mother is often also in a situation where there are no boundaries, because she is having to meet the needs of the "screaming mime" all by herself, and because her needs come last and the infant's needs come first, last and always.

Also, if there was damage to the mother during that time in her emotional development, and therefore probably for seven generations back, you are going to end up with some really big boundary issues because of the "developmental recapitulation" process that goes on as you parent your child.

Now the nine month old period is a turning point in the developmental literature, and it is called the "psychological birth of the human infant." This is the point where for the first time they are acting like a new-born colt.

They can crawl, they can get into things, and they start becoming a damn nuisance. They have a will and desires and intentions of their own and some motor coordination to be able to carry them out. So they get into the syrup and the coffee grounds and the baking soda on the shag rug and that sort of thing.

And so as the thing goes on down the line, you are going to continue to have boundary problems with the kid. "Where do my boundaries leave off?" becomes a major concern. What that means is, "Where do my rights leave off and where do the kid's begin?" And "Where does my identity leave off and the kid's begin?"

Boundary issues are really hard to define because of the one-way street nature of the parenting process and the constant demands and components that we have been talking about here. Questions like where do the kid's needs leave off and mine begin" rein supreme.

And if you were allowed no boundaries when you were in this period, you end up becoming blended with the kid with no room for your needs. That leads to depletion, exhaustion and resentment.

Or if you have issues on having your boundaries violated by the way it all went down for you when you were a kid that becomes what could be called a red hot issue. And then the kid picks up that and they react to it.

And the whole thing turns into a gigantic mish-mash of very confusing and upsetting things events and feelings, because boundaries are so difficult to know about, define or talk/think about. And the issue keeps coming up all the time.

Boundaries have to do with the complex interplay of all the needs of situations and of people and the processes of day-in, day-out, moment-to-moment parameters. And there are all kinds of practical problems that are involved in the thing also.

Like for instance, where do your, the child's and the other people in a restaurant's needs begin and end? What right does the kid have to express themselves when they are upset, and what about their needs? How many times do we have to stop at restrooms on the road? There are just tons and tons of boundary issues that come up.

THE ROLE OF EROS

Another gigantic issue that nobody ever really talks about is the matter of erotic feelings. Now Eros is the God of Love in the Greek tradition. It is also the energy of the creative, passionate, bonding, charismatic and connecting part of the second chakra -- all the juices. Oh and by the way, it is also the seat of sexuality.

With all of that involved in Eros, which is the foundation of caring relatedness between people, it is important to remember that physical sexuality is only one little piece of that. On the other hand, that piece is fully operative in any adult human being and nascent so in kids.

Any love relationship in which you care deeply about the other person involves Eros, and that therefore brings in the sexual component. So you have sexual feelings somewhere in the mix with regard to your parents.

You have sexual feelings towards your best friend of the same gender. You have sexual feelings towards your boss if you have a good relationship with them, and so forth. And you have sexual feelings towards your kids as a perfectly normal and necessary part of your committed relationship with them.

Another factor other than the sheer naturalness of it all is the fact that children are made to be incredibly attractive physically, emotionally and behaviorally as part of their high needs impact.

This is part of nature's way of keeping that "one-way street" from becoming a total burnout. The Eros intensity of the relationship is a commitment-elicitor and –protector, due to the child's being so damn rewarding, cute, sweet, real, caring, attractive, etc. That automatically activates our sexual reaction. And it is *not* a perversion! That is Love, period. It is no more "weird" to have a sexual reaction to your child than it is to have a sexual reaction to your best friend.

The task involved is to not be afraid of it, to not repress it, and to not "lose it" and act out on it. And if you are love-starved or if you have been neglected, distorted, violated or abused, you need to be especially vigilant that you don't fall into your damage with your kids.

This is unfortunately not at all uncommon, given all we have gone though. The *reported* rate of incest is now about 60%. Reported incest between mothers and children is about 15%, especially during the infancy period. Most of it seems to be impulsive and impetuous, rather than systematic.

Now unfortunately, that is a very serious problem because of the "in loco Deity" thing, because it means that "God raped me!" One woman had that occur when she was 6 months old during diaper-changing.

She saw her mother leering as she felt intense pain in her vagina. Her experience was that if she had been an adult she would have clove her mother in two in the total blind rage that infants get into.

Infants are essentially full range expressive people who have very undifferentiated responses to sexual invasion. The trouble is that an event like that stays with the individual in the form of homicidal rage.

What is happening is that the rampant selfishness of the collective consciousness over the last six and a half million years in conjunction with the isolation of the nuclear family has wrought havoc with our archetypes in this area.

On top of which, the deteriorating circumstances of the paranoid patriarchy, the Armageddon process, and the impersonal urban/industrial environment over the last several generations have resulted in an incest rate that is in effect astronomical.

Consequently, that is becoming one of the organizing experiences of practically everybody in the world at this point. It is, of course, one of the prime drivers to our putting an end to all evil as a mass phenomenon. We cannot and will not do this anymore.

By the way, Freud knew all about it. He discovered it in his first patients back in the 1890's. Then he started talking about it in the medical community -- in the midst of the Victorian era!

And he quickly realized his situation, as they were ready to ride him out of town on a rail and to destroy him politically and personally. He was, after all, a Jew in Austria. So he was forced to make a survival choice.

What he ended up having to do was to make the pragmatically imperative move to tell it in terms of what it wasn't by claiming it was in the dreams and unconscious wishes of his patients so that he could get the information out there, at least in watered down form.

The other piece of the involvement of Eros in child-rearing is when you personally are having sexual feelings towards your children. That is a fine, marvelous and loving thing to experience and be.

But what you have to do is to not repress it (which inflames it) and to not act on it because the kid can't handle that. But they can sure as hell appreciate your profound caring and admiration of them, which is what it all boils down to.

You *can* control your hormones! And you can handle it by some other means. But if you repress it, guilt-wilt it, get frightened by it, get enraged at the kid over it, or project it onto the kid, you are going to damage the kid permanently. You *integrate* it into a loving relationship with them.

The reality of the matter is simply that rearing children involves sexual feelings. It is just a part of being a loving, living human being. And do remember that kids have a very rudimentary version of it towards you too!

Unless kids have been thoroughly distorted by their early life history, they are simply enormously attractive, and they will remain so during their high demand period till they reach adolescence.

It is simply part of nature's way of giving some payback to the care-taking people. And that payback is in the form of loveliness. But it *does* put the care-taking people (and to a minor extent the kid) into a kind of complicated position unless you know what you are doing.

Now when you *are* aware of what is needed and you find yourself with erotic feelings towards your child, you just know that you are having a very strong emotional response to them, and you go find someplace else to handle this sexual energy, and you relate to the kid from the love you feel.

One of the really unfortunate things about this whole thing is that there is such a conspiracy of silence about it. As a result, most of us don't know this is happening or what to do with it. And then we get into all sorts of difficulties.

The reality is that you are going to get erotically involved in them. You can't help it. It is perfectly moral and normal to experience it, to appreciate it, and to sublimate it. That is all you need to do with it.

THE DEVELOPMENTAL RECAPITULATION

There is another phenomenon involved in child-rearing that needs to be addressed at this point. It is called the "developmental recapitulation," another one of those fancy terms from developmental psychology.

It is what you are doing while you are rearing kids from conception to the point where they leave home. You are in effect re-experiencing your own experiences at the same times all the way along as they go through their developmental stages.

This is not a conscious phenomenon, of course, but it does have a purpose. It is a "back burner" process that is designed to try to prevent your passing on the worst of what happened to you when you were growing up.

Now what do you think would happen if that were not the case? For instance, suppose there is a kid whose parent has a very low irritability threshold, who gets angry very easily. So every time the kid cries, the parent blows up and attacks the kid physically. And that then is part of the kid's formative process.

Now that kid becomes a parent. And because of that experiential history, they take it as the natural way of doing things that what you do when your kid cries is that you attack them. And three generations down the pike, you've got compulsive infanticide.

So what nature's way of dealing with this thing is the "developmental recapitulation?" So that you don't pass on the worst things that happened to you. It is like a selection process.

At the back burner level, you remember what it was like when that sort of thing was happening to you from your parent, and you in effect choose not to do that. This is the purpose of the phenomenon.

However, it is very complicated and difficult to know what to do with this situation. So we in effect fly by the seat of our pants, with the result that we usually do end up passing on the seven generations patterns.

We tend to be impelled towards doing unto others what was done to us. And so there is a pronounced tendency for us to basically pass it on because most of the child-rearing process is done on the unconscious level and by automatic pilot.

If you have ever witnessed the child-rearing practices of a younger soul crack addict mother, you know what I mean. The things that were done to her she does to them in spades. It is because of the fact that we are basically so overwhelmed under the circumstances that it is a "natural" process to do so.

Now the exception to that is the older souls don't do that. Older souls have more cumulative consciousness to draw upon and they have more capacity to retract and not pass it on. An older soul has vastly more experience, wisdom and capability. And that tends to come through.

As we move into the heart chakra, the whole seven generation pass on thing will in effect disappear, as there is no longer any necessity for our souls to learn from the "School Of Hard Knocks with Evil as the Headmaster."

So in the future, the intended purpose of the developmental recapitulation process to alleviate the worst of the past will happen normatively again, like in the commons period before we deteriorated in our functioning.

WHEN GOOD PEOPLE DO BAD THINGS

There is still another phenomenon that gets involved in the parenting process that is very disturbing and demoralizing to you as a parent, to those who know you, and to your kids. And that is when good people do bad things to kids.

Child-rearing is the hardest and most demanding/draining job in the world. And we get almost no training, no preparation, no resources and no supports for doing it because of the "kids come last" thing.

The result is that those who rear kids are put into an almost impossibly demoralizing situation. Consequently, parenting is the place where we are typically at our worst, in terms of our functioning capabilities.

So therefore it is not at all infrequent for an individual to be a very good person and to be very involved with other people, to be quite good at handling life, to be very good with their spouse, and to be very poor at parenting. Which is very confusing, alarming and demoralizing to the kid. It is very disturbing, and it leaves profound marks on a person's beingness.

Because when the child, the parents and witnesses can't see anything inherent in the parent's functioning to explain their bad behavior towards the child, everyone including the child will end up blaming the child for the parent's malfunctioning.

With the result that a kind of "magical thinking" ends up occurring in which the child has no idea what it is that they are or that they are doing, but that whatever it is, they are bad, wrong and evil -- and the parents are just reacting to that.

And that, in turn, sets off a whole chain reaction of events involving the child's trying to "put a new ending on the old story," first with their parents and then later with selective electro-magnetically attracted "stand-ins for the original cast."

This of course triggers an entire process of devastating patterns of relating, of ill-chosen partners, of self-destructiveness and of ecological damage that results from the individual's being convinced that they have consistently "failed to straighten out this thing with the "Home Office" (the parents in their head who they illusion conclusionally feel is God).

For they take it as God condemning them because of the "in loco Deity" process in childhood. They don't realize that what is really going on here is that the parents are doing unto others what was done unto them because they are operating out of pure desperation and lack of competence in this area.

The parents also tend strongly to defend their own self-worth by massive blame-throwing in reaction to their own bad parenting effects on the kids' functioning. We depend upon each other as our substitute for the lack of physical defense equipment described earlier, and we therefore go way out of our way not to lose our social support defense.

As a result, when we become isolated and self-hating, we are desperately defenseless. So we do whatever we can to "put the blame on Mame" so as to not feel utterly "unfit for human consumption." We are also desperate to avoid ostracism/annihilation. And this all becomes REALLY impactful in the "good person/bad parent" situation.

THE PARENTING CONTEXT

The reason that all this has been presented is because it is the background of how parenting has been done. This is the truth of what the processes and parameters are that you are embarking upon when you go to "do children."

Until at least middle childhood, there is a rather large imbalance between what you put into the child and what the child is able to give back to you. Yet at the same time, child-rearing is remarkably rewarding because of the biologic stuff of who children are, because of the fact that they are human beings with souls inside, and because they are the hope of the future.

Child-rearing is extremely important and rewarding in many ways. But by the same token, it is extremely difficult and draining, due to all the factors that we have been discussing here.

One of the things I had to learn about from the very beginning of my career as a child psychologist was what to do in the supermarket when I was a shrink seeing what a parent was doing to a child. I knew almost from the beginning that the answer is "nothing."

Given the circumstances of the way the world is arranged at the present time, if you try to intervene with that stuff, you are going to create a riot. It will also result in vengeance upon the child for putting the parent in a bad light.

You are going to produce the parent turning on you. You are going to have a non-understanding surrounding community coming after you. And it doesn't accomplish anything. So you swallow hard and live with it.

It is very difficult to rear children. By the time the process gets going, in most cases you are putting your oar into an incredibly complicated ecological system that you can't understand.

So basically, most of the time, there isn't a hell of a lot you can do. But at least with information like that presented here under your belt, you can have a general notion of what is going on.

And if it is your own parenting situation, you can at least try to do something about it. And perhaps with some circumstances with some people, you may be able to gently bring it to the parents' attention and to give them some assistance.

SOME GENERIC PARENTING PATTERN FAILINGS

What will be presented here are some of the patterns that have been found to show up in failing parenting processes around the world at this time. And the first one that comes to mind is the phenomenon called *selfishness.*

Remember that it was said here that up till now, we have basically been operating out of "What's in it for me?" as opposed to "What's in it for we?" as the primary criterion of how to operate.

And therefore, one of the prime problems that arise in the resulting overwhelmed, overloaded and non-supportive situation is that the parent comes to the conclusion that their needs are more important than those of the kids.

The basic rationale here is that the kids are dependent upon them, and they have to take care of their needs first before they can take care of the kids' needs. So that becomes a handy rationalization for rampant selfishness on the part of the parents.

The second generic parental failure pattern is the *"Papa/Mama knows best!"* In this process, the child has essentially no rights and no information, in their parents' eyes. This is a variation on the "child as cherub" stance. It is a form of radical harm-avoidance and an effective distrust of the child.

The third is the *"control or be controlled"* trip. This is a manifestation of the "kids are moral monsters" belief. The assumption is that they have to learn to be socialized and to have a conscience. The parents' experience is that children don't know any better than to be selfish, irresponsible, destructive and potentially harmful unless corralled in at all times.

Then there is the opposite, the *"rescue operation"* or the *"over-protective parenting"* pattern. They are constantly trying to prevent disaster to the kid. The reality is that this is insulting, possessive and demeaning. It sends the message that "You are a cripple." It is also a form of distrust of the Universe and of trying to out-perform God.

Another favorite is the *"not meaning what you say or saying what you mean"* trip. In this pattern, the parents try to keep things from the child, to engage in convenience-concerned parenting, and to be excessively casual in what they say around the child. They cause considerable havoc by not being truthful with the child.

Another common pattern is the *"sealed unit"* parent who has never had anybody in their life that they could trust enough to be able to let love in or to let love out. So they operate as an "urban hermit" in an "among us but not of us" manner. When it comes to rearing a child, there is little responsivity and receptivity, which results in "abandonment at an early age" for the child.

Then there is the *"manic-frantic"* parent who is trying to do it all – get the kid to their lessons and commitments while trying to work full time. There just isn't time for human relating and for their emotional needs or those of their spouse or their kids. They are in effect trying to do everything "perfectly," with no real regard for their ecological impact.

Next there is the *"Wipe that smile off your face, young man/young lady!"* orientation. This is the whole business of "What do you want that I don't know about?" and "What are you pulling off that I don't trust?" type of thing. Another aspect of it is the "When *I* was a kid, we had to . . ." and the "Since when did you have the right to have more fun out of life than I did?" stance.

Next there is the classic *"Because I said so!"* This is a unilateral assertion of their authority being laid on the child. It represents a kind of desperation on the part of the parent or it is an automatic pilot response without their even thinking. In any case, it is a manifestation of a power-down trip in which there is no respect for or sensitivity to the child's nature or needs.

A rather similar pattern to this is *"the Gospel according to Me!"* The parent(s) literally believe that they are the Final Authority on everything. In this one, the child learns that might is right and that power is the real basis of "morality."

Then we have *"projective identification,"* where the parent in effect says, "I just HATE that about you!" (As they suddenly turn the finger of blame back on themselves). In other words, the parent sees something in the kid that they built in and that they hate in themselves.

Still another parental failing is the *"pseudo-spouse"* pattern in which the parent puts their child in the role of being their spouse. They have done the "stand-in for the original cast" thing with their actual spouse, and they are desperate for love, resulting in their seeking spousal love from their child.

Then there is *"role reversal,"* where the parent senses the potentialities that their child has, and they put their child in the position of being the parent's parent.

Another very prominent process is the *"Peter Pan(ella)"* pattern where the parent wants to be "palsy-walsy" with their children because the parent won't grow up. They don't want the responsibility and accountability of rearing their kids.

Another one is the *"promises, promises"* or the *"dance-away parent"* pattern. In this one, result is a "my heart belongs to Daddy/Mommy" child who is forever hooked on trying to win over the withholding parent, and they end up doing unto others what was done unto them.

Next there is the *"will of spaghetti meets whim of iron"* situation where the kid starts to come forth as a force of will, and the parents end up with the kid running roughshod over them and everyone else.

Then there is the *"tantalizing tarantula"* pattern, where the parent is emotionally and sexually starved and they do the "seduce-slap" thing with the child. When the kid starts to make any kind of affection or responsive reaction to the parent's enticements, the parent suddenly turns on them.

Next there is the *"never good enough"* parent where no matter what the kid does or achieves, there is always something they DIDN'T do right about it. Like when they bring home five A's and a B+, they attack the B+. You are never good enough.

39

Then there is the *"envious/jealous"* parent who deeply resents their child's future life pattern and trajectory. They are deeply regretful about their own life pattern, and they either try to force the child into their own unmet dreams or they attack the child for their success.

Next there is the *"preacher's kid"* or the *"shrink's kid"* situation where the parent pours all their commitment and love into their flock or clients, leaving the kid unattended. This leads to the "heartbreak hotel" experience for the kid and to an out humiliation-inducing acting out response to the whole thing by the child.

Then there is the *"sado-masochistic minuet"* pattern where you have an effective "professional asshole" married to a "long-suffering saint." Everyone loves and trusts the "saint" and hates the "asshole." But what really is going on is that the "saint" is in fact a "mayhem mastermind" who uses the "asshole" for the so-called "saint's" sadistic intentions.

Then of course, there is the *"abusive cycle"* in which someone who believes they deserve nothing but the worst marries a batterer who builds up resentment, explodes, goes into remorse, wins the other parent back, and then starts building up again.

Next there is the *"betrayal"* situation where the pattern is in effect a "sell out" of the kid with regard to the child's needs, wants and desires over and over again. The child ends up unable to trust the Universe.

Then there is the *"fob off"* phenomenon, where the parents are neglecting, dumping and abandoning the child because they can't be bothered with the vulnerability and the responsibility involved in child-rearing, but who is so selfish that they can't let the child have a loving parenting anywhere.

Another one is the *"War of the Roses"* situation where they have reached such an impasse with regard to communication with the other gender child that it is in effect not possible for them to do so.

It represents such domination by their biologic gender qualities or by such massive sex role stereotypes that all connection and communication is effectively shut down. The title refers to a film about a complete breakdown of communication between a divorcing couple.

Closely related to this are two patterns: *"tripod-rage"* (the irresistible urge to kick anything with three legs) and *"cave rage"* (the irresistible urge to kick any opening). Both of these derive from the *paranoid patriarchy.*

Tripod-rage arises from women's fury at all of the injustices, exploitation and male failings arising from the operation of the paranoid patriarchy. It is something that starts with being built in from the mother to the daughter. However, her experiences with her father, her brothers, her boyfriends and the world at large consolidate it in.

Cave-rage is a bit more complex, in that it is the spin-off reaction to women's rage at the patriarchy and at males, starting with their mother's rage at them for being a male in a paranoid patriarchy. They find out they can do no right in their mother's eyes, and that they are in effect programmed to derail success in life because of that.

Their mother's situation is essentially a double bind, in that if she rears a successful male, she is generating a paranoid patriarch, while if she doesn't and she's raising a guaranteed failure that she can't respect. And the male ends up damned if he does and damned if he doesn't too.

And finally, we have the *"dissipation blues man/mama"* pattern like the crack addict with a dresser drawer for a crib. This goes with the other extreme cases like the brutal parent, the exploitative parent, the cruel parent, the psychotic parent, the psychopathic parent, the criminal parent and so forth.

The question that comes up with all these patterns and many others is, "What are we going to do about this?" We have in effect reached the end of the rope of the "School of Hard Knocks."

Pretty universally, the parenting process is leading to a generation-by-generation deterioration of manifestation. It is, if you will, the decline and fall of the Western Empire, comparable to what happened in Rome. It cannot continue in this way any longer. Hence the Armageddon process.

RECOMMENDATIONS

Now with regard to the business of how do you go about getting out of all these circumstances by trying to do something of a sensible process of rearing kids? There are several admonitions about this that can be put out here.

First of all, one of them is that you have to remember that *"They are not yours."* One of the reasons that this happens is because of the egocentrism of the world culture as a function of the average soul age on the planet. Another reason is the "selfish gene" biology of our species.

The net result of that selfishness is that we tend to regard our children as our personal property. In fact, the law still tends to hold that to be the case. For instance, there was a law in the statutes of the state of Kansas until 1925 that defined a man's wife and his children as his chattel, and he was given the right to "dispose" of them as he saw fit -- with all that implies.

The second admonition about children is that you need to be aware that *"They are not you."* Quite frequently, we get into the whole process of being mortified by what our kids have done or of totally wanting our kids to finish out our unrealized dreams.

Similarly, we want them to reflect well on us or we want them to have all the things that we never had. So we seek to force them to live up to our expectations and demands, without regard to what they want or who they are.

Another thing you have to keep in mind is that *"Your children are not your parents."* Often because of the extremely close, intense, intimate process of parenting, and because of the developmental recapitulation phenomenon, we start to put our parents' faces on our children. So your children are not your parents either.

Finally, *"Your children are not your destiny."* In other words, one of the things that has happened is that because of the fact that our life span has now expanded from about an average of 25 years in the middle ages to the later 70's as it is now, and it is going up to about 200 years according to solid medical evidence.

Under these conditions, the child-rearing span is going to change from almost all you ever do in your lifetime of 25 years to only the first part of your full life span. They are therefore no longer your destiny.

But we are still governed by our biology, by the human experiential archetypes over eons, and by the continuing cultural process that our entire destiny life purpose is to rear our children.

And so things like the belief that after they leave us they owe us, like the "empty nest syndrome," and like our desire for them not to leave us all tend to haunt us like "ghosts of Christmases Past."

The basic straightforward and simple fact is, though, that they come through us, not to us. Children are the generative principle in action, the process by which we contribute to the world of tomorrow.

Now in the past in the then division of labor, the female bore and reared the children, and the male created and set up the world into which these children were going to enter to carry out *their* destiny.

That is why the male is wedded to his work, because that is his generative function. It is his raison d'être, his reason for existence. Just like the mother feels that her kids are her reason for existence, the father feels that his work in building tomorrow's world is as important as the child-rearing process, if not more so.

Children should be regarded as somebody that we have been entrusted shepherding responsibilities for. We are here to bring them to the point that they are in a position to be able to cope with the world and with manifesting their destiny. And that is all we are asked to do. That is the approach you need to bring to the process of rearing children.

One of the most important things to keep in mind is that your children chose you. When we are out there, before we get in here, we plan out our destiny with our guides, including our astrological chart, which lays out the general course of our life.

That means that we get a sort of a general ballpark estimate of how the course of events of the major influences of our life is going to happen before we come in. Your chart doesn't say anything about how we will react to it or what we make of it or what we do with it. But it does give the lay of the generic land of what is going to happen.

It is kind of like you come out of high school and you go to the library and you pull out all the college catalogues. You fish around among the catalogues, and you decide which one you want.

Then you take the catalogue for that school and you decide what you are going to take your first freshman semester, second freshman semester, first semester sophomore, and so on. And that includes the professors, the times and the days, and all that sort of stuff. And that is what is meant by "they chose you."

They come in here to come through you in order to draw upon what you have, who you are, and what you will in all likelihood do for their purposes as a soul. And that may mean that they came through you to get abused as hell by you for their needs as a soul. If so, so be it. That's an unchangeable thing.

Another prime thing to keep in mind is the process of *"curds versus lemonade."* As has been said, one of the things that is an absolute guarantee is that you are going to blow it in some important way(s). It is just not possible to be human, to be in the space/time dimension, and to be in the world as it is now, especially with regard to the child-rearing process, without blowing it.

So what you do with that is instead of sitting there generating a bunch of curds from crying over the spilt milk, you get together with yourself and you start "making lemonade" out of the "lemons" you have created. That is the process and approach that you use.

When you discover that you have made an error, you own it, and you see what you can do to make something better out of the situation, rather than chastising and castigating yourself around the fact that you blew it. So what? We all do. We all have to. And that is fine. So what you do is to build from it for the benefit of all.

The second thing to keep in mind is the *"work with the purpose"* phenomenon. The fact that the daughter who gave me the feedback as an adult chose her mother and me to provide her with the programming she needed means that it was a job requirement for her mother and me to do what we did.

She had to spend the first part of her life being subjected to destructive influences and engaging in self-destructive activities in order for her sixth level mature soul to burn out her Karma until that was completed.

And then she was free to start living her life on her program of positive purposes that she also came in with. Which she has done. But until that Karma was burned, nobody could change anything about how she did anything or about what happened to her.

Regardless of what I did, regardless of what resources she had as a soul, as an ego and as a genetic system, and regardless of what anybody else did. Nothing made a difference because nothing was *supposed* to.

So because I was not as wise as I am now in my earlier years, I spent 28 years of agony over what happened to her until I came to the conclusion that when *"all the king's horses and all the kings men can't put them back together again,"* back off!

You are dealing with a soul-, destiny- and/or Universe-run process. You do not have the right or the ability to change it, so leave it alone. But that is after you have done everything you reasonably can. You try to change the circumstances, and when you find out that nothing works or that everything gets repeatedly undone, you honor their soul and their destiny design.

The first and foremost thing that you have to do when you are going to do the business of child-rearing is that you have to be aware of all the things that are involved in the situation at hand.

And then from that perspective, you open your heart to yourself. Get off you case and don't attack yourself over the errors you make. That's because that only makes you ultimately withdraw from the children or you attack them in the long run.

Open your heart to them and don't be afraid of your erotic impulses or your urge to kill. Don't be alarmed or enraged by the extreme drain and demands that are involved. That is just simply a part of the process. It is not forever or the only thing involved.

Furthermore, one of the other components of the inverted pyramid thing about child development is that the more quality you put into the beginning of their formation, the easier it is later.

If you go for the first three years with real quality input, the child profoundly shifts from a responsibility to a resource. It is a real royal payoff on your investment, so to speak. They become such an amazing human being when you do that. So hard work at the beginning generates gigantic gifts for them, for the Cosmos, for the community and for you for life.

So do the best you can with them, and don't harass yourself when you blow it. Make lemonade and enjoy the joys of the juices that result. Just plain shelf the self-castigation and the "Here is proof once again that I have blown it for sure" that we all more or less automatically are prone to do.

One of the things about psychotics that they have found is that their hallucinations are actually "tape loops" of the voices of Christmases past in the form of attacking parents telling them to do something destructive to themselves and to others.

Well most of us also remember vividly all kinds of nasty negative things that were said and done to us all throughout our formative process, because they were dramatic events that had great significance about who we are and what we think we deserve, especially during the "in loco Deity" early imprinting process.

So one of the things you have to be able to do is to open your heart to your parents and to your child(ren), and to be aware of the fact that they are human beings who started out as an innocent infant with a soul in there. And remember that they *will* respond very heavily to all of your commitment ultimately.

The next thing that is the kind of overall general principle that you want to manifest when you are investing in your child(ren) is to try to give them the fullest range of abilities that you can. The way I put that is, *"Open all the chakras."*

There are seven levels or components of the process of being a human being. And what your task to do is to try to expand on or to facilitate the emergence of as much of the capacities of their potentials as you can possibility do without killing yourself, enslaving yourself, or becoming enraged, exploitative, jealous, or any of the other stuff that can happen.

One of the primary processes involved in that is to seek to generate a balance between the *Yin and the Yang* in all you do and also in them. Yin is the receptive creative principle that shows up most concretely as the Feminine. It is the compassionate, holographically comprehending and juicy principle.

Yang is the initiative creative principle that shows up most concretely as the Masculine. It is the inspirational, mental, assertive, impact-making and aggressive principle in action.

Each of us has a different balance of the two, but each of us needs to have as much capacity to manifest both of them as we possibly can in order to be able to be an effective and full potential human being. That is another goal that you need to have when working with your child(ren).

The next thing to keep in mind about the whole process of child-rearing is to *respect* them. So what if they are having a hell of a time grasping some concept because of their immature physiology.

You need to respect them as a person and to respect their experience. One of the commonest mistakes we make is the "egocentric error." So here the kid is trying to master the concept of quantity in arithmetic, which is blatantly obvious to us.

We need to remember what it was like when *we* were having the same difficulty. We need to remember the degree of humiliation that is involved, like with the "nuggies" in the drive-in.

There is another story from my kids that is relevant here. Back in the early sixties when they were infants, we used to talk a lot about "goofing," and I used to say as I was changing their diapers, "Oh, you goofed."

Then I was told years later how they went purple with shame for their teacher when she said as she erased the blackboard on something she had written, "Oh, I goofed!" That became a burning memory for them for life.

Realize what their experiences are from *their* perspective. Their first experiences are the most vivid experiences, and they are basically going to remember everything for life almost photographically as a result. Know their experience and *respect* it.

Another thing to keep in mind is that they need *protection* as they move through their initial learning experiences in life. You need to protect them from the insensitivities of others, including yourself.

Therefore in this process of protecting them, you have to take into account all these ecological considerations surrounding their experiences. Try to acknowledge their experience so that you can respond intelligently with the kid so that they don't feel that they have in effect been abandoned by you in a parent-teacher conference, for instance.

Let them *express* themselves. Very frequently, we get impatient with their process of repetitiousness of communication and with the simplicity of their concerns as they first learn things. Their concerns are no less important to them than yours are to you.

Now that does not mean that you have to become a slave to your child's needs to express themselves either. This is a constant trade-off and problem-solving balance-seeking consideration-generating undertaking.

But one of the things you *do* need to do is to give your kids the chance to make a fool of themselves while they express themselves, because they are primitive in their skills, but they are *not* primitive beings.

It is very important that their expression efforts are validated and that they are being listened to with respect for their experience. Try not to do things like correct their pronunciation or their vocabulary too much.

As in the arithmetic example, it doesn't matter that the child doesn't know the difference between billions and hundreds and fifties. What they are learning is the various words and concepts of quantity.

One of the things we need to do is to seek to develop our capacity for tolerance, acceptance and the operation of the *neutral mind* when working with first time learners. The neutral mind is best exemplified by the old Chinese story.

In it some catastrophic thing has happened, and everyone around the farmer to whom it happened is saying, "Oh God, how awful for you! You must feel terrible." And the farmer shrugs because he knows that the story is not over, that the full import and meaning of the event is not in yet.

So when working with kids, stay in your accepting neutral mind awareness that the full import of the events are usually not known for a while. We have to make the best of the situation within the limits of our understanding of the moment.

You have to accept the situation the way it is, rather than getting all caught up in "What if?" and "If only" issues, which are only fantasy concepts that lead you to ignore the reality of "What is."

So the neutral mind is the process of accepting what is, of making lemonade if you have to, and of making hay when the sun is shining when you can. You try to avoid going into the fantasies of "What if?" and "If only" as much as you can.

Now of course, we are all human, and we can't help doing the "Big If" thing every once in a while. But when you catch yourself doing it, remind yourself, "Wait a minute. Where am I living -- in fantasyland or in reality? And what is the reality and what can we do with it at the moment to make this thing work the best way, given the circumstances right now?"

Now that brings up a lot of things that come under the general heading of *"the fair witness."* That is a concept from the spiritual realm that means your general approach is to look at what is going on, and you try to maintain some sort of objective recording attitude.

Otherwise, you get all caught up in what your agendas are, or in what you feel is going to happen to what you want to take place, or what would occur if . . ., and all that sort of thing governing your reactions to things. You need to take ALL of the data into consideration, not just your reactions to things.

One of the components of this process concerning the things that happens when you are not able to maintain the fair witness is called "LEWELLA." Let me tell you a little story here.

Here we have a couple of stones sticking out of the ground. And over here we have a bulldozer with a guy in a hard hat driving this thing. He is intending to push these two stones out of the way on his farm field.

But he doesn't know that what we have here is a huge buried dinosaur down here, and the "stones" are its horns. And it is pissed off as hell and it's about to come erupting out of the ground. A caption for this picture would be, "Leave well enough alone!" which is "LEWELLA."

What that means is that if you don't maintain some sort of detached awareness and common sense, you are likely to get yourself into some mighty big trouble with your plunging ahead pattern.

Another thing to keep in mind about the fair witness or *mindfulness* process is that what you resist will persist and insist -- often with very regrettable outcomes. You can count on it because you are putting energy into having your way about it without considering all the parameters involved in WHY you are resisting it and about what is going on inside you that makes you so insistent. This component of the fair witness is called *sensible acceptance.*

Still a third aspect of the fair witness is what is called the *"gifts in the garbage"* phenomenon. What this refers to is that every form of psychopathology and emotional difficulty pattern has the potential of bringing forth a genuine gift that would not be there if you had not experienced the garbage in the first place. It's kind of a "wiser but sadder" thing.

If you encounter a piece of garbage in your way of being, and you find that you are not able to shake it loose, seek to find out what the likely gift in the garbage is that is in effect its hidden purpose. That will likely take you out of the "resist/persist" dilemma, and it could lead to your garnering the gift.

This is in a way similar to the "all the king's horses" thing, where you are dealing with a soul whose destiny requires the problematic pattern. Keep that in mind when you encounter characteristics or processes that are going on that you wish weren't happening, but that seem to be impossible to change.

And here's another of the many things that come under the fair witness/mindfulness heading. It's called *"Shadow boxing."* The Shadow is those parts of us which were not allowed to be expressed or manifested when we were a child. As a result, we had to "shove it into the Shadow."

Because they are human and soul qualities that were not allowed to occur, once they get into the Shadow, they start to get all distorted out of shape. For instance, take personal potency as an example.

Many women are not allowed to express/manifest their personal potency because of the paranoid patriarchy. What happens to personal potency when it is shoved into the Shadow is that it starts turning into seething rage. What occurs with "Shadow-boxing" is that you start the whole process of cramming everything that is related to the Shadow-shoved quality into the Shadow, and you turn around and seek to batter it into submission.

And as a result of that, you get scared to death of everything associated with that quality in yourself and you avoid it all like the plague. And you also in essence enter the ring with it as you try to close it down and to drive it inside.

An example of that relationship to the Shadow is contained in an observation that a member of a spiritual group made about their white outfits. She said that Hermann Goering, Hitler's top aide, came up with great outfits for the Nazis.

And because that spiritual group aspired to be "pure white," they were "dancing in the white light," and because that means that you are prone to shove everything that isn't pure white into the Shadow, that indicates they had the potential of becoming a bunch of Nazis.

If you are trying to be something in a totally pure and perfectionistic (non-mindful) manner, you can count on it, the Shadow is going to get larger and larger, and "the Shadow knows . . ."

So don't do a misbalanced thing. Try to remember to be a fair witness with a neutral mind and a mindful approach. For instance, realize that everything is both Yin AND Yang, black AND white. Everything is a blend, not a purity. Try to make the thing work in reality, and strive to integrate rather than to shove things into the Shadow.

When you are working with your child(ren), seek to minimize the development of their Shadow by allowing them to be who they are, and by helping them learn from their mistakes in the process.

Also, teach them to integrate their Shadow stuff when they do end up unbalanced and excessively one-sided in their functioning. Model integration, talk about it, give suggestions, and give them encouraging consequencing as they seek learn how to do that.

Taking a moment to over-view this process that we are presenting here, it is clear that these are large attitudinal admonitions, because that is all you can do with regard to the business of raising kids.

It is what could be characterized as an Approach, rather than a set of specific recommendations for particular interventions or particular ideas (which have to be constantly contextualized in ad nauseum detail).

The general notion is to prepare them for living efficaciously -- with integrity, commitment and competence. The value system underlying it all is "What's in it for we --for Thee?"

Self-respect and self-provision, community commitment, and Cosmic congruence are the criteria of evaluation of all we do, all we intend, and all that results from what we do. Teach them to cope and to contribute in a manner that "walks the Walk" of the "Middle Way," the "Eight-Fold Path" of the Buddha by showing them the importance of handling every situation so that it is a Win-Win process and outcome.

And remember that parenting should be a *"leap-frogging mentoring"* process. That is, any mentor worth their salt teaches the mentee everything the mentor knows and regards as crucial for Right Living.

This automatically makes the mentee greater than the mentor, because the mentor melds the mentor's wisdom and skills onto those that the mentee brings with them, including at the soul level. The result is that the mentee comes away with more than what the mentor brought to the table.

And in the righteous process, the mentor then learns from what the mentee comes up with by their having integrated all that the mentor has taught them with what they already knew and were.

And after these two teaching processes are completed, their relationship shifts to be one between colleagues and peers. This is the working model of parenting that will lead to the best, most lasting, and most permanently expansive outcomes.

The next general principle is to *make sense*. That is, when you are doing anything, it should be congruent with your values, with their needs and with the requirements of the situation. What you do is in sync with what is happening, with what should happen, and what has happened out of coming from commitment.

One of the worst patterns that you can put on a child is what is common in alcoholic families, namely the "Jekyll-Hyde" syndrome. One day you get this, the next day in the same type of situation you get that arising from the cellar like a creature from the Black Lagoon. Especially when they are drunk. That kind of not-making-sense is devastatingly destructive.

Another way to put making sense as your guide is the imperative to *"be congruent."* That is, when you are doing anything, be congruent with what is necessary and fair. This means that you have to assess what is called for, moment to moment, making your behavior rather unpredictable at one level.

This is the opposite of "being consistent," which is a form of unrealistic rigidity. One of the things a lot of parents get into is the "Great God of Consistency." You know, the thing of, "You have to do this because you have to be <u>consistent</u> with children." What you really need to do is be congruent and to make sense with what you do. It is NOT a matter of always putting them to bed at exactly the same time.

Children require congruence. They don't require blind consistency. You are not running a boot camp or a military academy. You are seeking to rear a child who will live in the world as it is -- unpredictable, messy, complex, hard to control, difficult to understand and challenging to handle. They have to be able to think for themselves. The Christ once said through the Beatles, "Think for yourself, and I will be there with you."

Next, you need to *know their experience, to be aware of its impact, and to respond to that.* Like the thing about what it meant to them to go to the john in their pajamas. I use that as an example because it is so clear about what children need.

The reality is that *parenting needs to be a continuously conscious process.* It is NOT an undertaking that is done on automatic pilot. This because of the fact that we are likely to pass on our pathology and the preceding seven generations and all the other stuff we have been discussing here.

Basically, until we get to the point where we are a couple of generations down the pike and we are past this crisis period, parenting has to be an "up periscope" process all the time.

Sometimes you get overwhelmed, you get exhausted. You've got things going in too many directions, and you end up falling back on your automatic pilot patterns. But in general, the attitude and approach is to be aware of what you are doing at all times as much as you can. It is hard work, but it is the only way to break the chain of pathology that has gone back for thousands of years.

Think as you work with the children. Read about what you are doing. Share with others, and have them share with you about what is going on. Ask questions like *"Is this trip necessary?"* (Referring to what is happening at the moment).

Are you finding yourself saying things like, "Because I said so!" or "Wipe that smile off your face!?" Ask, *"What is the point of all this?"* "How did this happen?" "What is going on?" "What's needed here?"

And always the over-riding question that you can ask yourself and never answer fully is, *"What are they learning from this?"* That is the $64,000 question. Because, bottom line, that is what is what kids are -- learning devices.

They are building themselves for tomorrow. They utilize their every experience for that all-important concern and consideration. In the meantime, you are in the business of trying to serve and to be reasonably comfortable with yourself in the life that you are leading for and with them. So always ask what they are learning.

Speak to their soul, but honor their biology and their realities, particularly those of you who are old souls that have old soul children. Speaking with their soul goes a long way with such individuals.

But when biology requires that you do the sing-song voice or that you repeat the same story again for the six thousandth time or that you have to sit and listen to tons and miles and angles and numbers, you listen to them as you honor their biology. But at the same time, you have to be aware of what you are doing at all times. You talk to them like they are a person, because in fact they are, regardless of their age.

One thing that is important in this process is that you match both their soul and their being nature at the same time that you also match their biological nature at any given time in their life.

So though you are working with complex concepts in your head, out of your mouth and behavior come communications that engage them at their level of biological development, in terms of length of comment, wording, presentation and memorableness for their state of being and understanding at the time.

Now in terms of what to teach them, there are two very important things that are imperative that we convey to them. And those are 1) how to want well and 2) how to choose well.

We all have wants, we all have needs, and we all have desires. But the question is what is it that you and they are wanting, needing and desiring? Teach them to evaluate their own wants.

One of the most important processes of self-control and self-regulation is to know what is truly valuable and what is not. You give them feedback with regard to how to want well. And then once they have decided on what to want, they need to learn how to choose well so as to bring about the optimal outcome for themselves and for their world.

Of course, there is always the propensity to get into a whole kind of "object lesson" psychology intervention thing along the lines of, "You're not doing it right" or "Let me do it to show you how." And we need to be on the lookout that we don't fall into those kinds of interventions.

What is needed is a kind of "back burner" process where you are always aware that you are inculcating in them the ability to want and choose well. And that usually involves a lot of brief, pithy discussions of the parameters involved in the situation at hand, so that they come to look at things from the vantage point of what's really involved there. Choosing well encompasses all of the ecological, future needs, and other considerations that are the basis of good choices.

Another crucial quality that is required is to have a good *sense of humor*. One of the things about the business of child-rearing is that is often so damned serious. And one of the most powerful earmarks of successful parenting is a parent and child who are having an uproariously hilarious time periodically.

Clowning around, making jokes, seeing the humor in things, and the like are a corner stone of a loving and happy learning environment. Cutting up with hilarious bits of stuff yourself and appreciating and validating their efforts at humor are food for the soul. Humor is one of the primary processes of humanity and of healing. Be able to laugh at yourself, and at life, and to be funny. It's essential.

Still another thing that you have to do with children is that you have to provide a solid but sensible *structure*. They need structure because they tend to be impulsive learning machines, especially when they are younger.

Of course as they mature, you drop this structure back by degrees, because they start developing their capacity to function without "training wheels," so to speak. But when they are first starting out, they need those wheels.

Yet at the same time, the wheels need to be flexible, to be sensible, and to change from situation to situation according to the needs of the moment. The wheels have to be ones that make sense to the kid and that meet the needs of reality. And they can't just be convenience concern resources for the parents. They need to make sense to the child, to you and to the requirements of the situation.

So flexible, sensible structure is something that kids need in the early stages. As they get older they need less. But sometimes they need more because they are extending themselves a lot or because they are going through upheavals.

You may have to step in with flexible sensible structure again, even though you haven't had to do so for a while. That is part of the flexibility that is needed and part of the sensibility that is required.

The next requirement is the *"make and mend"* approach to relationships with your spouse and with your children. When you get into a hell of a hassle with a kid and they can drive you up the wall, especially with a favorite thing that they've found that sends you up the skimmer handle which they find very useful for getting their way, getting control, and getting revenge, that is the time when you need the "make and mend" orientation.

You have an issue and there's been an event with the kid -- say you blew your top. That's when you debrief and work with the kid afterwards about the episode so that you can make and mend your relationship.

You own your own irrationality and your own issues, but you also own their stuff and what they were doing. And you work out some kind of an attempt at a compromise with the kid. It may work.

But what's important here isn't so much the success of the compromise as it is the conveyance of the attitude of problem-solving, of commitment and of respect for them, for yourself and for the Cosmos. Own your own stuff, help them with theirs, and don't take it out on them, don't pass it on.

If you find that you are consistently blowing up at them or passing on something, study that for the patterns and issues involved. Pay attention to it, work on it, and own it with them.

You don't go, "Mea culpa! I have done this" with them. Just say, "I have this habit that I learned when I was a kid. I am having a hell of a time with it. And at times, you and I get into it over this. And I have to say that it is probably partly my fault. Now let's see what we can do about this."

The next recommendation is to *spend time with them* in whatever way that works. Kids don't really have to have razzle-dazzle thrills and chills kind of experiences every time you are with them. What they *do* need is you, your one hundred percent *thereness* with them. That could be side by side with them with you reading and their playing at your feet.

Spend time with them. It's very important. It doesn't matter what they are doing or what you are doing lots of the time, as long as they and you are sharing the experience and fully aware of each other.

Kids really appreciate shared experiences, shared time together. It is just a part of our nature. It doesn't matter how much time they have so much as what the quality of the time is. In other words, they need you there with them.

Quality time doesn't necessarily mean being in contact or interaction with them. It means being there with them, sometimes in contact and sometimes not. They need it, and they need a fair amount of it.

They don't need huge amounts of it though, even if they *would* love to have that much of it. But that's a preference, not a need. It is a matter that has to be balanced out with them in terms of the requirements of the situation at hand in the light of what you are doing. They are aware of such matters, and the sense of it will be apparent to them after a period of limit-testing.

The next requirement is that you *model integrity and self-respect* with them. That is probably THE lesson of today in terms of what kids need to learn. They have seen nothing but corruption and selfishness rampant all around us.

And one of the things kids need very badly to know is what integrity looks like in today's world in practical, doable terms that also involves self-respect and self-commitment as well.

Seek to model integrity with them and self-respect in everything you do, because it is going to be the "bottom line requirement" of tomorrow's world. Selfishness doesn't cut it anymore, no matter what.

Another attitudinal approach thing is to run your life and your parenting on the basis of *"no regrets."* Remember what was said about the curds. Basically, you make the best choice you can at the time.

And then you find out with new information coming in that changes the import and impact of what you did. Instead of sitting there worrying or hassling yourself about that, what you do is just simply to make a new decision. New information, new decision, no regrets.

This is called *"no shame learning."* In other words, guilt as remorse for what you have done is a realistic response. But shame for what you are or what you *should* have been doing or done or what you would have been or might have done is not helpful or realistic. Simply choose again.

When you are working with your children, your goal is to figure out as best you can what their purpose is, and then to *facilitate their destiny.* Remember that's the thing they came in to do in here. Seek to help them along.

By the time you have been with them for a while, it will be fairly clear something of the nature of what they are here for and the direction they are going in. What you want to do is to enable them to do that as much as possible. After all, they came through you, not to you. They came through you because they wanted you as their teacher and launch pad for their purposes here.

Help them with it, even if that involves the "king's horses back off." Let them be themselves and to manifest their purposes. Let them be who they came here to be and to be different from you, better than you or less than you if they have to.

Also, let them evolve in directions that you would never take. It is after all *their* destiny, not yours. They are evolving into a world that we don't know about yet. And usually the young have a better idea of something of the nature of where things are going than we do, because they are planning and working on putting themselves into that future.

They have a natural attunedness and sensitivity to the future. Not always accurate, but better than we are able to do.

At the same time, your child-rearing involves the business of being concerned about and working with the *kinds of people* that you find your children attracting, selecting and bringing home.

If they are bringing home sickos, start to work with your children about that around why it is that they feel that they have to have sickos in their life. Not in the accusative sense, but in the sense of what kind of people they are associating with and what that means about their relationship with you and with their relationship with themselves. Look into how that that might be corrected -- make lemonade.

So let them evolve in directions that you wouldn't consider because they are after all running their own show, and they have a different job that you do. You can't of course, let them walk right off a cliff. But on the other hand, don't try to get in there and control everything.

Another big one is to let them *grow away*. Remember, they are not your destiny; they are only coming through you. Your child-rearing process is going to be an increasingly small proportion of your life.

You are not the be-all-to-end-all of your children's lives. Make your <u>own</u> destiny and as much as you can arrange it, build your own commons. Pick people who are high quality that you can trust your kids with, and work with trying to bring them in as a part of your community-supporting network. That includes day care centers, schools and classes of various kinds.

Your children are human beings who are here to live a life of their own. When they reach the point where they have achieved majority and they want to leave, let them go. Don't get caught up in the empty nest syndrome. Make a new life for yourself, now that phase one is completed.

QUESTIONS, COMMENTS, OBSERVATIONS, AND CONCERNS

QUESTIONER: In old souls relating to younger souls, and in adults relating to their own inner child, do all the same parent/child concepts apply?

LINCOLN: Mostly, except that one about talking to the soul of your child. If they are a younger soul, they can't handle the sort of thing that we were talking about here. So you basically have to rely on what you could characterize as more biologic norms for a younger soul child. The younger soul is the mover and shaker of the world. They change things. They definitely have a role and a contribution. They are not lesser beings because they are younger souls. They are learning a different set of lessons, and they have a different destiny, another role in the world to play.

QUESTIONER: They are not children? A younger soul is not a child?

LINCOLN: No it is not.

QUESTIONER: It is a fully formed adult.

LINCOLN: That's right, when they've grown up. When you are dealing with a young soul child(ren) and you are an old soul that is one of those things with the king's horses. You don't try to produce an old soul destiny for that kid. You honor the fact that they are going to be a mover/shaker in the world, and that they are going to be out for power, money, prestige and those kinds of things. You honor what their purposes, values and motivations are, and you try to support them in making the right choices as best you can with the amount of advice they will let in. You basically honor biology and respect their destiny with them. You don't use the old soul training process with them. When you are working with your own inner child, you have to basically deal with it in whatever terms your own soul age requires.

QUESTIONER: When you talked about the LEWELA theory back there, what is that monster you are talking about that you are supposed to let alone?

LINCOLN: What it amounts to is one of the things that we tend to do is the right and righteous thing. We think we know what is going on, so we rush right into acting on that.

LEWELA means back off and take a look at the larger situation. The question here is, "Is there one of those intervention at whatever costs impulses involved here?" It means to take a good look. It is a part of the neutral mind thing. Try to check out as much as possible before you make your moves. Sometimes it ends up that after you have looked at everything, you realize that there isn't a hell of a lot you can do. Sometimes you realize that you *can* do something, but that you have to do it in a different way.

LEWELA means leave well enough alone until you know what you are dealing with.

QUESTIONER: You're not referring it to the subconscious Shadowing where you shove things down not by choice usually, but say in an abused child situation. Children -- all of us -- push things away that we don't look at. In parenting, when you are talking about some of the situations like the sado-masochistic combinations and the unspoken messages, those are things that occur in giving guidelines -- and we can all learn these things.

LINCOLN: One thing you have to be aware of in the sado-masochistic minuet is that there is an unconscious process going down and they are going to fight to the death to maintain that system.

If you are working with a kid or a family like that, you have to be aware that you are in deep and you have to back off. That is a strong LEWELLA kind of thing.

What you do is to work with the kid or the family with arm-extenders to avoid getting maelstromed into the system. And if you are working with a kid in such a family, you deal with the situation by very careful and subtle coaching.

QUESTIONER: If you are that coupling, then there has to be an unconscious effort to manifest that constellation?

LINCOLN: Oh yes.

QUESTIONER: Then to rear a child, those unspoken messages are out there. All of these processes you have talked about to better raise a child are memorized, and sometimes it is not understood where this well-spring of behavior is coming from.

LINCOLN: When you notice the same things going the same way over and over again, you look to see what they are, and you pay attention to that to get some sort of handle on the process.

QUESTIONER: What if that LEWELLA thing is that untapped information that has to be realized.

LINCOLN: That's right. You have to look at that carefully because some of that stuff --

QUESTIONER: You need a guide. This is psychological. This is not just spiritual.

LINCOLN: That's right.

QUESTIONER: The psychologist's job is to cut out for them in the future what you are talking about for this big change.

LINCOLN: It is also a part of your own child-rearing process. To the best extent that you can, be aware that this is the situation that you are facing and remember the context of all of this stuff and be easy on yourself.

If you have a consistent pattern, notice how it works. See what you can do to work with it. Just the knowing of it radically changes the situation from the kid's point of view.

You may not even have to say anything. Just your awareness of the fact that you have a tendency to do this helps.

QUESTIONER: You are speaking as if an adult automatically knows that. I agree with what you are saying about respecting the child and understanding the level that they are coming from.

But as an adult, I don't think adults with all these complications are capable of rearing a child without psychological help.

LINCOLN: That's right. The point I am making is to remember the batting 300 and to make lemonade. Do the best that you can. That is all I am saying.

The general approach to the thing is to try to move on it from this attitude that we are talking about, but be aware that you are up against some pretty intense stuff, including your own neuroses which are built in as part of our training process and destiny.

And so you work the best you can with what you've got. That is a kind of a general approach you would take, as opposed to automatically doing the thing without thinking or getting all over yourself because you are doing it. You just try to make the best of it.

Bit by bit, that helps. You can't do a total reorganization of the entire thing because that is your life, and it is your circumstances. There is so much varied stuff and all that sort of thing.

Bit by bit, you work on it. That helps. It is the attitudinal thing rather than any particular technique that matters. Just the approach to try to make the best of the situation is the attitude that works.

If you have a lot of handicaps and the kids already have neuroses and what not, you make lemonade as best you can. Remember, we are biologically designed to have the circumstances we are for the purposes of the way the world is at this time.

QUESTIONER: The concept is that the child would pick an abusive situation to manifest themselves.

LINCOLN: Like in my daughter's case, she chose it so she would be able to burn Karma. In many of our cases, we chose it so we would learn great skills about the nature of the way the world is and how to deal with it against these odds, and then we would begin to generate the "gifts in the garbage," and we would start to be contributory at that level when the circumstances allow it, which are coming.

It is the "story's not over yet" kind of thing. Be aware that the destiny decisions and the soul processes are very complex. You have to be aware that sometimes you will know something about them and sometimes you won't.

But one thing is clear. The soul and the Universe process is *not* crazy. They do what they do for some sort of purpose. You have to figure it out. But at least you know that there is some purpose to it, and you try to make the best of it.

QUESTIONER: The gifts in the garbage sound good.

LINCOLN: It is.

QUESTIONER: I am a little bit uncomfortable with that theory, that someone would choose an abusive situation. That sounds like an adult having an indictment over a child.

LINCOLN: In the sense that they chose this so they deserve this, that kind of thing?

QUESTIONER: Yes.

LINCOLN: That is not the kind of thing I meant. The thing is that what happens is that when you are dealing with a circumstance that is not the absolute best for the kid, be aware that one of the components of the situation is that the kid's soul knew exactly what it was doing at the level that it was doing it on, and it therefore is going to use that for some purpose of its own.

And that is a state of affairs where you don't then say, "Well, you made your bed, now lie in it!" And you don't beat yourself up for having "caused" it (you implemented it for the kid's soul).

You just get into wondering what *that* was for. "I wonder if we can make anything better out of this situation." It is a kind of attitudinal approach.

QUESTIONER: I was wondering about the concept of that. I was asking what that concept meant and where it comes from. It is a religious concept? Is it a spiritual concept?

LINCOLN: It is *not* a religious concept in the sense of how religions usually work. It is basically a spiritual concept. It has to do with the reality of what we are, which is soul beings. And basically we utilize the vehicle and our lives for the expansion of our soul and the expansion of the Cosmos.

We do it in all kinds of funny ways, especially when we are younger souls still learning the ropes of Cosmic coping. As we get older as souls, we are basically teachers.

We use practically everything we do to teach ourselves and to teach others when we become older souls. There is a whole lot of information around about that kind of thing. That is not some off-the-wall flaky thing. It is part of a larger context.

We are at the beginning of an avalanche of comprehension of the Cosmos, finally. Like after all these many, many millennia where all we knew was that there was this thing called a soul.

Now all of a sudden we are starting to get a lot of information about how this stuff works. We are as yet just at the early trickle stage of this. We get things like this we are discussing, but we don't get a lot of context info yet. But over time I think we will.

As we go through this evolutionary process of consciousness growth, we are going to get a hell of a lot more understanding about how this all works.

We are only kept in the dark as long as we need to be, if you follow what I mean. As our collective consciousness moves up into the heart- entered thing, it also moves up into much more spiritual/secular integration kind of stuff. That is another thing that is coming in the near future.

Things are changing drastically all over the place. That kind of information will begin to make more sense to us. I was just talking to somebody during the break about what does it mean, "I am that I am?"

That is a phrase we have heard a lot. It basically turns out to be one of those phrases that goes into 30,000 Cosmological things, and God knows *what* it means. We are getting some information on that. There will be more as time goes by.

What are the parameters and dimensions that determine what a soul chooses in the way of its curriculum here? We just don't know much about that.

QUESTIONER: That is metaphysical.

LINCOLN: Yes. We will find out some day more and more about that, but right now we don't know much about it. We do know one thing. If you have a very strong predetermined destiny and intention like that, and you try to change that, you are going up against a lot of brick walls, and you are going to create a lot of pain for yourself.

We have to sort of work with that to see if you can't make the best of the situation like I did ultimately with my eldest child. That is all you can do.

QUESTIONER: Thank you.

LINCOLN: Anything else?

QUESTIONER: I don't know if I want to ask this now or to get into this at this point. I ask this question so that maybe everybody can respond for a future now.

The overview I have gotten from you is like a simplified stage theory which is pre-three and post-three. Post-three being apart from the terrible twos and that type of thing. Post-three seems to be a gradual unfolding of consciousness and spirituality.

LINCOLN: Also a whole set of things around enculturation and elaboration and integration. It is quite a complicated thing, but there is much more environmental involvement by that point.

QUESTIONER: That is being contrasted to the point of people I know who would view things like pre-puberty and post-puberty to be much more important.

LINCOLN: I know.

QUESTIONER: I see where childhood kind develops slowly from zero up to whenever puberty is now. And after that, it is a completely different approach. Everything is a new ball game.

LINCOLN: There is a lot of physiological change that happens there. But there is also one that happens at about three and another one at around six. And most of us have not been aware that so much happens so early and is so important.
That is the latest information from developmental psychology over the last twenty-five years. It is brand new stuff. That is why most people are not aware of it.

We are beginning to find out a great deal about how this works now. Much more happens in the early stages than we ever knew. What I have given you is the latest scoop, so to speak.

The other stuff, the long-standing wisdom of the past, is also true. What we are doing is adding this on as new wisdom to put with what we already know to make us more capable of integrating all this stuff as we go along.

QUESTIONER: It may have been a matter of emphasis, but I am coming away from this session interpreting you as kind of not putting that much difference between a five year old and a fifteen year old.

LINCOLN: Oh, no. There is a hell of a lot of differences. There is a whole lot of stuff that goes on in between there. But that involves a whole other lecture on developmental psychology.

QUESTIONER: I am bringing this up.

LINCOLN: Very good point. I am glad you did. I appreciate that. What you are saying essentially is that what we have been talking about tonight when I was commenting in the beginning about the business of how the child-rearing process develops, we were talking primarily about the first three years.

But when I am talking about the overall parental attitude, it covers everything from conception all the way to the point of departure from home and beyond.

It is the attitude with which you approach the thing rather than particular developmental milestones that are going on. That would be a whole other lecture on how do you deal with the kids who are five years old or eight years old.

There are a whole set of developmental processes and phenomena that we know about that are very complex and very real. This lecture is about a kind of new slant to bring to bear on all that.

This is definitely not, "You've got it by the time you are three and that's it." What is true is that a whale of a lot of foundation-laying occurs by age three, and then there is the next stuff about what is happening later on.

For instance, as you well know, there is a huge brain change and a bunch of body changes that happens during adolescence, where, for instance, they become fully sexual beings. That changes everything of what they are and how you work with them.

Tonight's lecture was more like a general approach to how you go about parenting for all child ages. Anything else? That was a good one. All right, we can go home.

PLAY IT AGAIN, SAM

This is a discussion of one of the most emotionally loaded and important periods of development in childhood, namely the span from age three to age seven. A tremendous amount of personal evolution and formation occurs during this profound period. In order to understand it though, we have to go back and describe a bit our evolutionary process as a species.

As you know, we evolved from primates who have a troop structure with a very strong male dominance pattern. They are interdependent, and the rearing of the young is done primarily by the females, but the whole troop participates. They are a cohesive unit that looks out for and looks after each other for survival and fulfillment purposes.

Now things got a great deal more complicated when we became ensouled and human. But the same general social design held. This meant that for many millennia as we did the hunter-gatherer thing, the "village" was a large campfire site surrounded by marked areas for individual families -- and all of it was very temporary, like a camp site.

Everyone shared the common ground, and the children were everywhere, under the supervision and tutelage of whoever was present. Everyone considered it their prime responsibility to rear the children, and the "in loco parentis" phenomenon reined supreme. As a result, everyone considered every child their child, in effect.

This meant that everyone knew each child intimately, and the child experienced the whole spectrum of human manifestation. The village grouch was compensated for by the village love and whatever the biologic parents didn't have, someone else did and the parents had things no one else did.

As a function of this process, the whole village participated in the formation of every child, and they all knew what each individual child's proclivities and resources were by the time they reached age three. At that point, the child was assigned to be apprenticed in some culture resource-provision process, such as the tool-maker, the warrior, the cook, the artisan, etc.

After four years of apprenticeship and intensely interpersonally focused training, the individual was now an adult who was fully prepared to function as such in the tribe. There was a great deal of social interaction during this period with their peers and with the adults in the group. This resulted in the flowering of their sexual and societal role and process in a free-flowing but supervised environment.

Now seven may seem awfully young for functional adulthood, but you have to remember that it was a very simple tribal culture they were acquiring and operating in. Also, the average life-span was about 25 years. It is for this reason that the Catholic Church made such a big deal of "the age of reason" -- seven years.

So this is the basis of our "hard wiring" regarding the learning of how to be a human being in a societal structure. The very beginning was a society-wide undertaking, and the introduction and induction of the gender and societal roles were handled from age three to age seven, during the individual's "apprenticeship" period. And it was also society-wide in its handling.

Now fast forward the tape to the present. What has happened is that what used to take up to 250 people to do now is expected to be handled by two or even one person. Furthermore, it is done in a context where kids come last in our priorities, due to the ravages of the patriarchal societal structure.

Needless to say, this is an overwhelm situation that will have to be changed as soon as possible. We are indeed going in that direction, as the whole of humanity moves to the heart chakra, and the culture of the "Enterprise" becomes the basis of our living process. As Captain Piccard said in response to being asked by someone from our time what they do about money, "We don't -- we just do the best we can for everybody."

Meanwhile, back at the ranch of how things are now, the situation during the age three to age seven period has been characterized as the "Oedipal" and "Elektra" period by Freud. These are two ancient Greek plays about disastrous play-outs of this period resulting from patriarchal patterns.

In other words, under the conditions of the isolated nuclear family situation, the process of enculturation our children into their appropriate gender and societal roles is now fraught with severe difficulties with often destructive outcomes.

This is because of the massively demanding requirements of the situation in such a child-rearing context. In our culture today, the isolated nuclear family is in a progressively debilitating situation.

The pragmatics of the family's context requires that the family members provide each other nearly all of their love and commitment. At the same time, all non-immediate family sources of such inputs are pretty much denied to the adults in the family. They are seen as "potential affairs," "more willing to spend time with the guys," "more interested in your gal friends than your kids," etc.

Modern realities also require that all the other needs of the family be almost exclusively met from the resources of the spouse/parents. Thus, all the survival necessities, the quality of life provisions, the learning resources, and the parenting and caretaking responsibilities have to be somehow dredged up from within the personal resources of the two adults in the family.

This overload of demands and under-supply of resources takes its toll on every family sooner or later. One of the major crunch points of this process is the amount of energy and time the individual family members have available to them to provide for each other.

One of the common situations that develops is where there is an all-but-inevitable competition between the various life-support activities for the time and attention of the people involved.

For instance, earning a living competes with the need for strokes and involvement. The needs of the other family members for support and caring competes with both the need for earning a living and for strokes, as well as the need for alone time. And the demands of quality parenting pull them in still another more or less mutually exclusive direction.

In addition, a similar competition develops between the family members for their life-support supplies of strokes. "Sibling rivalry" among the children, between the adults, and between the adults and the children results.

The fact is that there usually is just not enough time, energy, love and commitment to go around. Not to mention the matters of the amount of competence in each of these areas, or the degree of freedom from neuroses and relational issues that greatly muddy the waters and compound the difficulties.

Then add to this the tremendously loaded issues for the kids of the working out of their gender identity and role, and you get a profoundly complex and difficult period of personhood development for the individual and for the whole family.

One of the really major accomplishments of this developmental stage is the working out of what their gender means, and what kind of gender role identification and expression they are going to work out. This is particularly difficult nowadays, with our rapidly changing conceptions, standards and folkways. It is also especially challenging for those whose sexual orientation is for the same gender.

Sexuality and the customs and taboos involved in it are fascinating new discoveries for the child. At the same time, this ties in with the love-deprivation issue and the identity-formation process.

This results in things like "favorites," and in the beginnings of the "Daddy's little girl" and "Mommy's little man" relationships. (Incidentally, notice the infantalization of the female and the premature empowerment of the male in these cultural cliches).

The issues, processes and parameters involved in these developments are greatly intensified in families where the spousal relationship is not effectively meeting the needs of the adults for love, which to say in nearly every family. It's even more compact and loaded in single parent families.

Now what happens under these conditions is that all that was covered by the whole of society in our pre-history has to be now handled by the individuals in the isolated nuclear family.

This means that for all intents and purposes, the parent of the other gender becomes the only cultural representative involved in the formation of their gender identity, sexual manifestation and societal role.

And of course, it is even more difficult an undertaking when there is only one parent and gender role manifestation available. Under these circumstances, the child has to turn to non-parental figures for their other gender capability development, or they have to reach inside the single parent's psyche to draw upon the yang or yin qualities that the parent has inside.

There are three primary things that have to be accomplished during this three to seven year old period. The first is the activation of the latent qualities of the other-than-bodily component of the soul.

That is, it is a time when the individual has to provide themselves ways of manifesting the part of the soul that is not given by their bodily structure. This means that the boy has to find a way to channel his soul's yin qualities, and the girl has to develop her soul's yang potentials.

And the way this is done is by doing a Ph.D. dissertation type study of how the other gender does it. This means that they become utterly fixated on and fascinated with how the parent of the other gender functions.

Or they become highly sensitized to how the mother's animus (her male within) expresses itself or how the father's anima (his female within) manifests itself. They are in effect absorbing like a blotter every aspect of the other-than-their-bodily-gender process in their target person's functioning.

The second thing that happens at the same time during this period is that the child becomes intensely tuned into, responsive to and desperately needy of extremely fine-grained feedback from the parent of the other gender or from the yin or yang component of their target person's functioning. In other words, their target person in effect shapes their expression of their bodily gender characteristics during this time.

Human interaction takes place on two levels at once. One of them is the overtly accessible and comprehensible stuff that takes place in "real time" -- the things we can understand and see.

The other occurs at the rate of sixteen interactions a second, which is too fast to be seen or controlled, but which forms the foundation of massive amounts of feedback and information-transmission arising out of social interaction.

It is primarily at this sixteen times a second level that the yin or yang manifestation provides the crucial feedback to the child on "how'm I doin'?" with regard to how to be a graceful woman or how to be a noble man.

That component of their target study person's reactions that packs the wallop of the other-than-bodily-gender responses to the individual's manifestation is the key factor in the evolution of the person's gender role manifestation.

Finally, while all this is going on, a third critical developmental function is occurring. Now this fixation/fascination process places a great strain and drain upon the targeted parent.

It is as if the child affixes themselves to the parent's leg for four years. That is a tremendous demand, one that would effectively wipe the targeted person out if there wasn't some sort of energy compensation.

And indeed there is. Have you ever noticed how utterly irresistibly gorgeous kids of both genders are from three to seven? It is particularly noticeable in photographs taken during this time period. And it is universal in its appeal -- both genders are compellingly attractive to both genders of all ages.

What is happening here is that Eros is in full bloom during this phase of the child's development. That is, all aspects of the second chakra -- passion, charisma, connection, bonding, caring, zestfulness, joyfulness, creativity, projection, eroticness, etc. -- are activated to full potency.

Everything, that is, except genital sexuality. They are too young to handle that, and they are not physiologically able to comprehend its expression. Indeed, being targeted in that manner feels to them like they are being raped by God, due to the "in loco Deity" thing that is happening at this time, where they take everything that happens as God's gospel truth from the horse's mouth -- the Source Itself. It is part of the process of absorbing an entire culture in a few initial years.

So what happens during this highly demanding and draining period is that the child emanates the "juices of the Cosmos" -- Eros love. And that, in turn, is highly rewarding and rejuvenating for the targeted parent. It keeps them going, and it allows the child to be intensely demanding and invasive as they conduct their dissertation study, and as they learn how to do it right as a man or a woman.

However, it also adds a huge complication and confounding effect to the whole process at the same time, in two ways. One of them is the fascination factor about the difference that makes a difference.

Although they are not usually sexually activated during this time, they *are transfixed* by the other gender's characteristics and qualities. And of course, part of that transfixedness focuses on the physical difference between the child and the other gender.

Now in the case of the boy, the most obvious and salient difference towers above him most of the time, as he stares in fascination from below. It is only when his mother is sitting down and he is in her lap that he has a chance to try to explore that fascinating difference by unbuttoning her blouse.

But for the girl, the situation is far more difficult to deal with. Especially in our culture, where the fly outlines the Big Difference right at her eye level all the time. This has the effect of constantly stimulating her "magnificent obsession," and she therefore bugs him about wanting take showers with him, sitting in his lap and squirming, etc.

Now remember, this is occurring in the isolated nuclear family, where there isn't a whole community of peers and others to guide them through this process of exploration in a healthy and enhancing manner.

The people in the isolated family are effectively "running on empty" a lot around all manner of fundamental human needs, with no real resources outside the family to meet them.

Under these conditions, this Eros-loaded fascinated/fixated gorgeous child is a really loaded stimulus for all kinds of extremely powerful emotional reactions. Unfortunately, as we are finding out now, all too often, disastrous trouble develops right here in River City as a result. Yes, Mom's involved too, either by collusion, by set-ups, and/or by acting on her overwhelming feelings herself, especially during the infancy period.

But even when things are copasetic on this front, there is still the tremendous loading this whole situation has for the entire family. For one thing, you have this demanding little "stalker" seeking to take up virtually all of their targeted person's time, energy and involvement. That has quite an effect on the targeted person, but it has an even bigger effect on everyone else in the family, spouse included.

Perhaps spouse especially, although the siblings have quite a sibling rivalry reaction to all this, and the extended family and the general public really react to the "inappropriateness" of the child's behavior and focused concerns. Nevertheless, it is the spouse upon whom the bulk of the impact of all this lands.

In the case of the mother watching her daughter take her husband away from her, it generates a lot of female competition and abandonment-paranoid reactions. She goes into both counter-appeal moves on her husband and "bitchy pissed off" responses towards her daughter.

She and her daughter are apt to get into quite a "dance macabre" during this period, establishing an unhealthy relationship with other women. It may also precipitate seductive-destructive modes of operation with men in the daughter.

But the really biggie of this nature is the husband's reaction to his son taking his wife away from him. Remember, we are a "primate dominance hierarchy" organism in a paranoid patriarchal society.

As a result, the father is apt to go into lethal combat/competition with his son, and all the complexities of the Oedipus complex come into play -- fear of castration by the father, to-the-death combat/competition reaction to all males by the son, territorial defense, "crotch-notching," etc.

And of course, this IS the third function of this whole period. It results in the child's having to balance their passion with their concern for the ecology and for Cosmic correctness. In other words, it triggers off the built-in capacity for a conscience that requires this kind of all-consuming situation to activate it.

In the community child-rearing situation, all of these factors also operate, but they are handled in an enhancing manner for the most part. The result is a healthy resolution of all these conflicts and the successful operation of the three outcomes in the child. But in the isolated nuclear family, this period often goes off like a nuclear explosion. It produces the conscience, but at a considerable cost in damage and distortion of development.

And that brings us to the title of this little oddesy. Because in the confines of the isolated nuclear family, this process often does not resolve well. And that, in turn, creates the circumstances where the individual is compelled to try to put a new ending on the old story with stand-ins for the original cast. Freud called it the "repetition compulsion."

It also results in our being 100,000 volt electromagnetically attracted and compelled to marry the stand-ins -- with often disastrous results. This being because we are pulling in repeats of our parents at their very worst. This produces a divorce rate of 50% on the first marriage, 75% on the second, and up in later marriages.

Unfortunately, for younger souls, this can get to pretty ridiculous proportions -- like Elizabeth Taylor's eight marriages. But on the other hand, older souls *do* learn from this process -- either within a successful first choice (despite the Oedipal/Elektra component) or in subsequent relationships.

And fortunately, we are *all* going into being more mature souls, as the whole human race enters the heart chakra. This means that both the isolated nuclear family situation and the reaction patterns that create this kind of outcomes are leaving the scene forever. It remains to be seen how this will play out, but more mature souls will definitely find workable ways to make it happen. So the future looks very bright indeed.

In the meantime, it behooves us to bear this information in mind, so that we can do what we can to alleviate, heal and enhance our situations within the restrictions of our present culture. It *is* do-able, and it is critical for our health, welfare and happiness that we do so.

BUZZ-BUZZ

Have you ever noticed how gorgeous kids are from age three to age seven? They become Shirley Temple and Little Lord Fauntleroy -- utterly irresistible to both genders. There is a very real reason behind that besides the generalized thing of the child of being so cute that we are willing to put up with and are compensated for the tremendous demands and one-way street input that childhood requires if the children are to acquire an entire culture, personality and destiny equipment in a very few years.

We are primates, and primate young are expected to be fully functioning by three years of age. As we evolved through the hominoid to the ensouled human thing, we extended the learning period to seven years.

That's why the Catholic Church talks of the "age of reason" -- seven years. We have brain-matured and experienced enough by that time to be a functioning adult in a simple indigenous culture.

Now this more than doubles the maturing/learning time for our young, and it puts a hell of a drain demand on our resources as parents, as a community, and as citizens. So nature came up with a complex compromise, as she always does in such situations. And that compromise was the tremendous attractiveness and bonding-elicitation that children develop from age three to age seven.

In the indiginous culture, everyone in the community (about 250 people) participated in the child-rearing process. That meant that the whole group felt full personal parental responsibilities and privileges with all children.

That resulted in the *in loco parentis* phenomenon where the child, the older person in their presence/vicinity, the parents, and the community all agreed that everyone was the parent of all children, functionally speaking.

This made it possible for the parents to be citizens as well as parents -- they could have a life of their own while rearing their children. Everyone recognized and honored the special biological bond between the actual parents and the child, but everyone also accepted the responsibility for care-taking and educating every child in the community.

This meant that the village curmudgeon was compensated for by the village love, that someone would have what the parents didn't have, that the parents would have things that no one else did, and that the family bond was supported and made workable.

One of the really important effects that this process had was that everyone got to know each child really well in the first three years. And at age three, the community was quite aware of what each child's natural inclinations and capabilities were.

As a result of that know-ledge, the children were then apprenticed from age three to age seven to learn the role in and the contribution to the community that they were going to manifest their whole life. They would be trained as a tool maker, a warrior, a basket maker, a plant-gatherer, a cook, etc. And they entered the community a fully trained contributor at age seven.

Now this sounds strange until you remember that we are talking about a primate life-span of something like twenty-five years here. Also, we are talking about a kind of quasi-permanent "camp ground" lifestyle around the large fire at night, etc.

Things were pretty basic and manageable by a seven year old in such a culture, and a twenty year old would be quite adequate and appropriate as a "tribal elder" who has been there and done that over and over, and who therefore has life wisdom to impart to the community.

During this three to seven adulthood-apprenticing period, the child had to learn the technical know-how they were going to use all their life. But they also had to learn how to be an effective member of the community, and that meant learning all the gender role requirements, the community member requirements, and the capacity for self-regulation and responsible/considerate functioning. And the teacher and the community continuously trained them in how to do these things during that period.

Things went like this for about six million years minus ten thousand. That was when we went from hunter-gatherer tribal to agricultural village in our functioning. That put a tremendous change on us as a necessary evil in order to evolve to where we are now.

Primarily, it separated us from each other a great deal, forcing us to develop individualistic ways of handling things for the most part. But our biology did not and has not changed. We are still wired to be reared by a whole community in the manner described.

What happens as a function of this is that in the isolated nuclear family, one to three individuals now have to accomplish what it took 250 to do all of our biologic history. And we have to do it in a vastly more complex culture that has extended the learning period to what used to the life-span of the species! The inevitable outcome is a lot of difficulty in carrying out the parental role, along with the resulting distortions of the biologic programming process.

And that becomes particularly problematic during the age three to age seven periods. When Freud started his work in psychoanalysis (he was a neurologist and in his fifties), he found that his patients were suffering from severe effects of that period of development.

He therefore formulated that neuroses occur from that time. And he was right -- up to a point. Subsequent work now indicates that the real action occurs from the very beginning in the womb, and that the child is core-formed by age two to two and a half -- just in time to be apprenticed into the culture.

And therein lies the rub. For instead of parents, a whole community and a mentor to train you in all the things that are required for full community citizenship, all we have now is the parent(s).

But our needs are still there, and this period of child-rearing therefore becomes rather extremely intensely demanding. And that is where the biologic compensation for all the mentoring that has to be done comes into action.

What occurs is that during this period, which Freud called the Oedipal period for boys and the Elektra period for girls, the second chakra or the emotional body really activates the Eros energy -- the biologic juices of love that shows up as bonding, connection, creativity, passion, commitment, charisma, attractiveness, and relational lovingness.

It does so in order to provide some profound energy and motivation to keep the parents, mentor and community going during this very demanding period. But the resulting impact on the isolated nuclear family all too often activates the patterns found in the Greek tragedies that Freud talked about with the titles of this period for the two genders.

What the child has to learn during this period is essentially three things, to be discussed in a moment. The rest of what used to be learned during this period in the hunter-gatherer culture now being learned at a later period of development, where the child's relationship to the community, the Cosmos and their destiny/contribution are acquired over a much longer period.

Incidentally, childhood was only identified as extending past the seven year old period in the industrial era, adolescence appearing only after the First World War, and youth appearing only after the Second World War.

For instance, I read a book published in 1960 in England in which one of the first chapters was devoted to the proper caning (you heard me) of six month olds. That isn't cruelty, though cruelty certainly results from it.

What it is, is that thing about our presuppositions about who children are. To the traditional Brit, a child is an unsocialized adult. Now imagine an adult acting like a six month old. What you get is an irrational primitive psychopath. So you start instilling responsibility and community commitment from the very start. Leftovers from our evolutionary history.

Now back to the Oedipal/Elektra period and that irresistibleness thing. What the child has to learn in that period is, as was indicated, three things. The first is "the other half of their soul manifestation."

What is meant here is that the body provides all the necessary equipment for the expression of that gender's qualities in the DNA. But it does not provide it for the rest of the soul's characteristics and qualities that are the biologic domain of the other gender.

So the individual has to apprentice it with the parent of the other gender. They in essence have to do a Ph.D. thesis on how the other gender does everything. They therefore become obsessionally fascinated and fixated on the parent of the other gender.

They glom on to their leg and won't let go for four years, so to speak. They are biologically driven to notice, study and emulate everything they can about how the other half of the human race does it.

Now this puts a hell of a demand, constraint and drain on the parent of the other gender. And that is where the activation of Eros comes in. The child becomes irresistibly attractive and endearing.

This provides some juices as compensation and motivation for the targeted parent. However, it also generates a tremendous responsiveness on the part of the child to the "buzz-buzz" -- "vivre la difference!" energy of the cross gender relationship.

Not to the point of full sexual manifestation, because they don't have either the physiologic equipment and condition nor the experience to be able to handle and manifest that. But everything else that is involved in a love relationship is there full bore. It makes for a whale of an attraction between the two individuals that keeps the learning process happening.

However, it also generates a "difference fascination" in the child, and they forever want to explore and examine those differences. The boy wants to unbutton his mother's blouse, and the girl to take showers and baths with Daddy, at an obsessional and seemingly addictive/insisting level.

This is made all the more difficult by the tremendous emotional charge and flattering impact that this lovely creature of the other gender being that interested in and fascinatedly demanding towards us creates.

This particular aspect of the situation is a little easier for the boys than it is for the girls, because the object of most of his fascination is located quite a bit above his head on the caretaker, lifeline and ultimate God stand-in. Meanwhile, for the girl, she is at just the height that the physical object of her fascination is at eye level and arms reach all the time, and his fly is right there.

On the other hand, it is a lot easier for the mother to deal with a horney toad little boy than it is for a father to deal with a femme fatale seeming seductress. This, combined with the horrendous inequities, distortions, oppression and damage done by the paranoid patriarchy that has accompanied the last ten thousand years of our evolution, produces the hideously high rate of incest, sexual abuse and misogynistic destructiveness that we have been subjected to all this time.

Due to the cruelty to women involved in the patriarchy, the same factors also produce a lot of cruel seductive-destructive behavior from mothers to her sons, though not nearly as much physical incest and sexual abuse as between father and his girls.

Nevertheless, we used to think that babies were like sacks of potatoes, and mothers didn't hesitate to play with the penis as a result of this and her hostility towards males in the patriarchy. The result is that males have much more sexual abuse damage from infancy, while females have it from the three to seven period.

Now let's look at the situation of a father dealing with his glommed-on-to-his-leg Shirley Temple. He is being required to meet her demands, intrusions, invasions and fascination-driven insistences and tantalizing/arousal-generating investigations for four years.

He comes home from work and he is instantly attached to by a gorgeous but incredibly draining daughter. And then the chemistry thing starts happening due to the Eros energy, and he has to deal with his very unfatherly feelings.

Furthermore, he starts having what therapists call "transference reactions." What that means is that there are only three people who impact him at this level of intensity and potency -- his mother, his wife and his daughter.

Now since we all recapitulate our own development as we raise our kids, he is back to about three to seven himself, and the result is that all of the feelings he had towards his mother at that time come back and are transferred to his daughter.

And that includes his Oedipal feelings, his desperation for the love he never got from his mother, and his homicidal rage towards his mother (normal at age three and resulting from his mother's usually repressed but potently subtly acted out hostility toward him as a male).

It is this, in conjunction with his massive damage from the patriarchy and his daughter's Eros-driven fascination with him that so often leads to the sexual abuse phenomenon we see.

And it seems to be getting more intense (though not more frequent, as world-wide data are now telling us). So we see the terrible incidence of sexual abuse and its disastrous outcomes.

What is happening is that the patriarchy and the whole world order that was required up to now is leaving, and it is scaring the hell out of everybody, with the result that we are doing a "last grasp" -- on our own air hose -- as the patriarchy dies out so a new level of human development can occur. It makes it crystal clear that we can't go on in the old way any more, period, end of report.

Incidentally, a word of reality needs to be put in here. Which is that most fathers manage to keep their cool enough, either by withdrawal, pushing away, or somehow using his consciousness to deflect all this, that they are nowhere near the prime offender in the sexual abuse thing. That "prize" goes to the brother(s), followed by the grandfather and the family friend, roomer or whatever. Fathers come in fourth as the offenders.

Meanwhile, what about mother and her Little Lord Fauntleroy? As was said, she has a lot of things going for her that the father doesn't in this situation. One of them is that she is the one who determines whether sexual or closeness events are going to occur for the most part.

This is due to our long primate history of the sexual process being initiated by the female. It has been found in studies in singles bars, for instance, that it is the *female* who sends the initial interest stimulus (often very brief and subtle but highly potent), to which the male reacts with what appears to be uninvited approaches. So she has control of the situation from this, and the mother's function/role/relationship power base with her son is enormous.

Furthermore, the whole physical set up is wrong for the boy on the exploration/examination front. He just doesn't have either the stimulation or the opportunity to do the blouse thing very often.

And she is his God figure to boot, because kids put God's face on their caretakers until about age three/four. He wouldn't DARE act on his fascination/fixation most of the time. So this situation is one in which the mother does have the glommed-on-to-her-leg thing, but not the sexual activation thing for the most part.

What she DOES have is the whole double bind of rearing a boy in a paranoid patriarchal culture. If she shapes him into a successful male in the culture, he is a patriarchal prick and she hates his guts.

And if she doesn't do so, he is a loser and she hates his guts on biologic betrayal grounds -- he's not a real man. What that does to her is to put her in a position of having her "tripod-rage" (the irresistible impulse to kick anything with three legs) constantly activated by her son, but especially during the Oedipal period.

And then he comes at her with the sexual exploration/examination obsession/fascination, and she has a golden opportunity to use her position of power and sexual potency to release some of her rage in slyly subtle (and usually unconscious) seductive-destructive and vengeance-vendetta behavior towards this demanding, invasive and boundary-violating little patriarch.

And as was indicated earlier, HER sexual thing is much more activated during the intense intimacy and handling/fondling that occurs during infancy. It is here where she recapitulates her longing for caressing love that she rarely got as an infant, and she then puts that together with the tripod-rage thing and the sack of potatoes thing to act out her love-starvation in a patriarchy, her rage at males, and her greatly stimulated sexual system.

Later, during the Oedipal period, the massive amount of physical contact and stimulation are no longer happening, and so she is much less likely to become sexually abusive on the physical level towards him, even though he is gorgeous. She DOES, however, react to him with great amounts of elicited sexual feelings on the psychological level.

What he more usually gets during the Oedipal period of three to seven is a lot of transferred hostility from both the imprinted tripod-rage from his mother and her reaction to her father's usually patriarchally badly mishandled management of the Elektra period and its tremendously damaging effect on her, along with the unavoidable attraction to him and whatever that activates in her, such as her seductive-destructive tripod-rage and patriarchal double-bind things.

Now for both genders, this all boils down to a horrifying "fact," which is God is doing all this to them. Remember kids put God's face on their caretakers till around age three or four.

So what in effect happens is that boys in infancy and girls in the Elektra period get raped by God, so to speak. And furthermore, they also get hated by God due to all the processes we described above.

The result is the worst possible outcome -- hostile, violating and sexual rejection by one's Creator. It leaves massive scars. Kids can survive and even thrive at times if the circumstances are right in war zones, and they can even handle death and violence. They adapt. But sexual/rage stuff kills their spirit and sears their soul. It takes a long, long time to recover -- if ever.

It is important to remember at this point that all of this sort of thing was defused and diffused in the hunter-gather period (though the primitivity their consciousness and lifestyle led to other major problems).

The whole community was available for providing parental modeling of how the other gender does things, and for handling the obsessional/fascination exploration/examination thing.

It was not concentrated on one individual with a "glom-on-to-their-leg" thing. They weren't nearly as conscious as we are, but they didn't have to deal with what we have had to either.

What is crystal clear at this point is that we simply HAVE to make major changes in our whole value system, culture and consciousness to break out of this downward spiral of inter-generational deterioration of manifestation.

And we are in the process of doing just that with the Armageddon thing, which is designed to be a "Cosmic boot in the butt up" to the heart chakra, where we trade in the fear that we have been living with as we learned the ropes of coping in 3-D for the love that is the true nature of the Cosmos and the foundation of all real relationships of any kind.

We are going to "graduate" to the next level of learning, which is love-based, not fear-based. We will continue to be challenged, but no longer by the "school of hard knocks" with evil as the headmaster -- "evil" being "live" spelled backwards.

67

We have wrung that rag dry, and we are now going to be hit with expansion-producing challenges instead of regressive-reductionistic challenges by primitive consciousness beings.

And we will then have a culture in which we can entrust our kids to the community again, as the *in loco parentis* thing returns. Only now on a vastly more sophisticated and committed level. That is where all this pain and suffering as the patriarchy collapses is taking us.

This completes our discussion of the first task/accomplishment that occurs during the age three to seven period -- namely the learning how to manifest the other gender qualities so that aspect of our soul can express itself and contribute during our sojourn here.

Next we turn to the second thing that needs to be going on during this period. And this focuses on the other gender parent's responses to the child above and beyond what we have been talking about here.

Now research has demonstrated the human interaction takes place on two different levels at once. One is the one we are familiar with and can do something about -- namely the kind of events and communications that take place in "real time."

But there is another simultaneous communication process going on. This one takes place at the rate of sixteen interactions a second -- which is beyond consciousness and control.

It is a biologic foundation of our nature, present in the womb. If things go awry here, it means that we get continuous messages that are destructive to us -- and nobody is the wiser about it.

For instance, there was this film clip taken from the research that demonstrated all this. It is five minutes long and it shows a mother holding her identical twin sons, four months of age.

On her left arm was "her fav" and on her right, "his fav" (the father's favorite of the two boys). In real time, they both squiggled and wiggled like infants do. About a minute and a half into the film, "his fav" started fussing. That's what you see on the real time event level.

Then you watch it in slo-mo, and you see that she and "her fav" hare have a love exchange going sixteen times a second. But she and "his fav" are having a rejection exchange sixteen times a second.

After ninety times sixteen rejections (1540 in all), his face starts to distort, and then you get to watch a man's life unfold before your eyes. Because he is receiving that rejection from the God figure from the very beginning, and that will carry into the rest of his life, with profound effects.

What this has to do with the issues of this discussion is that the second task/accomplishment that should be going on during the Oedipal/Elektra period is that the "buzz-buzz parent" is required to be providing feedback to the child about how to go about being a successful person of their gender.

In other words, the mother is required to teach her son at the rate of the automatic pilot sixteen times a second feedback/interaction level how to be a noble man as only a woman can teach him due to her intense sensitization to this and to the power of her reactions and inputs on him. And the father is required to teach his daughter how to be a graceful woman as only a man can teach her, due to his potent subtle responses to her.

Now this is a really heavy requirement of the responsible parent because of all the unconscious concentration that has to go on during this period in how they respond to and initiate with their child on the automatic pilot level.

Now this is a "natural," in the sense that it is the normal and biologically programmed response system the parent has built into them. It doesn't require thinking about it. In fact, thinking about it is a very good way to mess it up completely. It is far better to just do what comes naturally.

Or rather that is what is required when all other things are working reasonably right, like in the indigenous cultures of yore. But remember what we are dealing with here in the isolated nuclear family, as we discussed above.

All these factors combine with whatever neuroses and cultural glosses the parents have to create all kinds of damaging messages at the sixteen times a second level, instead of a large preponderance of appreciative reactions and corrective responses that move the child to their appropriate gender manifestation.

What is required here to correct for this once we know about it is to work on our own healing around the kinds of wounds and reactions we have going in the involved areas, such as our attitudes toward the other gender, the patriarchy and our cross gender parent.

That has the effect of hugely changing the automatic pilot sixteen times a second messages that are being sent. As was said, it is better to let this "trickle down" rather than trying to control yourself at that level -- which can't be done, and which would only compound the problem.

Also hugely ameliorative and corrective is what has begun to be called "conscious parenting," in which you let information like this sink in and you put out the intention to do your level best to meet the child's real needs (and your own) moment to moment to the best of your ability and within the restraints of each situation.

Of course you will make errors and fall short, but then you do a "no regrets -- I did the best I could" and a "make lemonade out of the lemon instead of creating curds in the spilt milk" thing.

Anyway, all of this puts another tremendous demand and drain on the "buzz-buzz" parent. It is a huge responsibility, and the kid is biologically driven to extract the best they can from you about this need for subtle shaping.

Unfortunately, what usually happens here is that the parent is so overwhelmed, repulsed and/or rageful that they don't do anything like the kind of job that is required. To make matters worse, all the other stuff and the parent's personal neurosis really compound the damage. And this leaves the child will all kinds of massive self-worth issues, other gender relational issues, and gender manifestation issues.

It is probably largely for this reason that there is such a sharp increase in the homosexual orientation. Normally about 1% of the population is homophobic by soul choice -- they want to have a loving family relationship with a person of the same gender as a soul learning experience every once in a while, going all the up the soul age experience or soul age ladder.

But when the culture is crashing and burning, the child-rearing is so disrupted that another 9% join the honest homophobic out of hetero-phobia and hetero-fury. This is why psychiatry is having such a time with the issue of whether homosexuality is pathology. Homophobics are NOT pathological, but all the hetero-phobics and hetero-furious are. And that's 90% of the group.

The last time there was that much pathological homosexuality was in the decline and fall of the Roman Empire. It is another part of the ending of the patriarchy and the onset of the heart-based world.

That brings us to the third special learning process that is going on during the "Oedipal/ Elektra" three to seven period that adds itself on to the other overload of parental responsibilities in the child-rearing process in the isolated nuclear family situation.

And this one involves the whole ecology ultimately and basically. Because what is required in this third learning/task accomplishment is none less than the activation of the conscience.

Now what that means is that the processes for acting out of conscience are biologically built in, but they need a "releaser process" to activate them permanently during this period.

Now this part of the process involves the child learning to balance their passionate obsession about the "buzz-buzz" parent with the requirement to be ecologically concerned, caring, committed and contributory -- to have a conscience.

And the way it works is that their massively demanding and ecologically impacting process inevitably generates strong reactions in the people in the environment -- the other same gender parent, the siblings, the extended family, the circle of friends, and the general public.

Blouse-unbuttoning or lap-squirming elicits quite a reaction, for instance. So do excluded and extruded siblings to all the special treatment the child demands during this period and the amount of attention/involvement they get from the targeted parent. So does the same gender parent to having so much of their spouse's attention, energy and time/resources being forcibly devoted to this child.

Now the situation and process by which this happens is both similar and different for the two genders of children. Let's start with the girl's situation/process first. Here we have the girl demanding Daddy's time, focusing excludingly and extrudingly on him, being fascinated with his "differentness, with all the resultants it generates," living out of the "Daddy is God and can do no wrong" experience, etc. Now what is going on in the environment that is unique to her situation?

What is involved here is that the mother is repeating her own emotional experience at the same age, and so she is operating on two levels at once. One is her responses to the situations, processes, events and issues that this period brings up regarding her relationship with the child, with her husband, with her sexuality, with the ecological impact it is all having, with her mother, with herself, and so forth.

And the other is her reaction to her own childhood and herself, and to projectively identify with her daughter, so that she does unto the daughter what was done unto her at that age, and so that she acts out her deep hatred feelings about herself towards her daughter. She is also dealing with the devastating attractiveness of her daughter and her own moving out of that phase of the female life cycle at about the same time.

So the mother is having quite a lot of complicated reactions to her daughter's developmental process. She is envious, jealous, mother-hatred projecting, self-hatred projecting, harm-avoidant ecological protection reactions, deprivation-experiencing, and of course, her own personal neuroses.

Also involved intensely here are her reactions to the patriarchy and what it has done to her and what it might do to her daughter. All in all, it is quite a loaded mixed bag reaction. And it all comes at her daughter at both the automatic pilot and the overt levels.

It is this mixture of profound processes that lead to the "where's Mommy?" phenomenon. What is being referred to here is the question of where was she as such things as inappropriate over-involvement, withdrawal or pushing away by the father, and/or sexual abuse were going on towards her daughter.

Inevitably, due to all of the deep-seated and often unconscious processes involved and to her own major wounds from this period, she will tend to "tune out" or "turn away" or even attack the daughter if the daughter seeks her help in the situation if it is going badly.

So to summarize what is happening to the daughter as she "buzz-buzz's Daddy," she is going to get a lot an envy, jealousy, deprivation and ecological harm reactions from the world around her.

She is also of course having whatever experiences her father or other male significant other is doing with her and its effects. And she is getting whatever responses and reactions she gets from her mother.

Out of all this, she has to come to the conclusion that she has to track her ecological impact and to consider both environmental and cosmic issues about how to keep some semblance of balance, fairness and rightness in her functioning and effects on the world around her. And she learns this from all of the reactions she gets from the environment during this four year period. It almost always results in her ending up with an activated conscience.

The son's situation is rather more complex due to the testosterone effect and to the evolutionary history of our species. Remember, we were primates, and their social organization is composed of what is called the "primate dominance hierarchy."

Being a little more realistic about it, it comes out as the "meanest son-of-a-bitch in the valley" and his henchmen, with his henchmen playing "king of the hill" and "kill the king" in a constant competition and combat process -- all to show off to the ladies, who are critically evaluating them for their value as providers and protectors.

Now what that means is that when the son goes into "buzz-buzz" with his mother, his father is going to really react in the long biological history-based competition-combat reaction.

So while the son is having to juggle all the processes, responses and interventions he is getting from the mother and the environment around all the kinds of issues discussed for the daughter, he also has to deal with the "King-Prince" thing.

This is a profound biologic heritage thing where he is hard-wired to try to topple or at least out-do or match the king, and the king is equally hard wired to protect his position and possessions -- including his wife.

And this REALLY intensifies the conscience-elicitation process. Since males are run by yang energy and testosterone, they are driven to make an impact, to change things, to leave legacies, to make a name for themselves, etc.; they have to be particularly concerned with ecological and Cosmic issues.

And the tremendous battle format that permeates their relationship with their father, no matter how it is expressed, really ups the stakes involved in the Oedipal processes with his "buzz-buzz" mother. Because "Big Daddy" is there with his big stick along with everything else. It usually operates as a very intense and deep opening of the conscience.

As a result, males tend to be both more simplistic about conscience issues and more concerned with them than girls are during the Oedipal period. Girls usually have to take a little longer after this period to find out what the costs and conscience issues are for their behavior, as they refine their social skills by cruel rejections, gossip, manipulations, etc.

Boys become very principle- and rule-dominated right after the Oedipal confrontations and conflagrations. And the Oedipal issues tend to stay with them the rest of their lives, both in regard to their relations with women and intimates, and especially in their relations with other males and with the ecological/cosmic basis of things. True, they can completely lose all contact with this, but at their core, it is always THE big issue due to the intensity and importance of this developmental challenge for them.

After this period is resolved in whatever way it is, the next step is for the individual to take what they have put together and put it out there in the world, as they explore where they stand in that larger arena.

Then school, peers and the larger environment, along with the development of all their success skills or not, become the big focus of the development process. After all, they have now become a full-fledged member of the community, biologically and evolutionarily speaking.

To pull all this together, then, what we have in the three to seven period is the enculturation and apprenticeship process for the person's becoming a member of the community.

It is a journey fraught with difficulties and intense challenges to all involved in the isolated nuclear family. It is again a tribute to the resilience and fundamental decency of our species that we got this far despite it all.

We are now heading into a radically different world in which the community will again become trustworthy because we are all moving into the heart chakra. Not without resistance and trauma, but in all probability successfully in the next few years. This will hugely unravel the complexities and traumas of this period of child development for all involved, thank God.

"OH MEIN PAPA!"

      This is an exploration of that strange creature called "Father." Due to the massively distorting, even dementing and demonizing effects of the paranoid patriarchy, we know remarkably little about the fundamental nature and manifestation of this crucial masculine process and phenomenon.

      What we have instead are all the "father failure" outcomes of the roles and myths forced upon us by the requirements and restrictions of the paranoid patriarchy process. The need is for both a non-patriarchally twisted and clear understanding of fathering. The basic attempt here is to "de-mystify" some aspects of what fathering is and does.

      It could be said that the father is the "magical male" in our lives. He manifests the Masculine for the first time in our experience, and he sets the template on what we can expect from the Masculine for the rest of our existence. Who he is and what he does therefore has life-long impact and import, for better or for worse.

      There are several factors that need to be explored in order to understand what fathering means to us, and how it influences everything that happens in the human condition.

These factors are:
1) Cosmic/spiritual/soul.
2) Biologic/evolutionary/genetic.
3) Guiding drivers/universal experiences/archetypes.
4) Cultural/historic/ethnic.
5) Contextual, personal, experiential/situational.

COSMIC FACTORS

      The primary, foundational Cosmic element is the manifestation of Love in action. Everything one does must reflect and express That of which the Cosmos is composed, and That which is the basis of everything. This is the foundation floor of Fathering.

      It is a "Win-Win Universe," ultimately, albeit with "win-lose" and even occasional "lose-lose" processes along the way to the final positive/expansive outcome. Love is the essence of everything and everyone, and it must be manifested at all times. And Fathering is no exception.

      The second Cosmic factor is compassionate caring, respectful acceptance, and coming from the Heart. Knowing that we are all "chips off the Old Hologram" and that everything is a conscious being, it is crucial that we honor and care for the essence inside every expression of All That Is. Working with the welfare of everything is the quintessence of the Cosmic element in action, including Fathering.

      The third fundamental Cosmic factor in Fathering is the Yin/Yang Principle. The Yang is the creative initiative process, and the Yin is the receptive creative process. In other words, the Yang gets things going and sets the direction of things, while the Yin works out the implications, ramifications, applications and manifestations of what the Yang starts.

      The relationship between Yang and Yin is a team-working co-creative process, and the Yang carries the responsibility for initiating well. Yang is visionary and results-seeking, and it therefore operates as the leadership influence and position. It is the generative principle of the male -- the looking out for the needs of today and for the building of the resources for tomorrow.

The Yang also operates with Nobility and Honor, and it sets and enforces the values and standards by which things are evaluated and implemented. It manifests fundamental Integrity and Responsibility, and it is guided by the Authority/"Senex"/Wisdom factor. The Yang is the inspirational and larger vision component of who we are.

Authority is "earned respect," and it is based upon a consistent "track record" of Wisdom and committed contribution to the Cosmos and to the community. An Authority also manifests and instructs in True Values and good judgment. It has the courage of Cosmic convictions. An Authority is admirableness and exemplification manifested -- a "gentle giant," like "Yoda" or "Captain Piccard."

The Yang is also Power personified. It is the impact-maker and the challenge-seeker. It has "Dominion" -- the Rulership Principle -- and it makes sure that all the needs of the Realm are met in a Cosmologically and ecologically correct manner. It also manifests Strength, Endurance, Dignity and Persistence in the execution of Its influence.

The next Cosmic factor that is operative in Fathering is humorousness. The series "Conversations with God" demonstrates beyond any reasonable doubt that God is what you could call "Funnier than a rubber crutch." Along with being a positively expansive spiral, the Cosmos is also full of fun and funny bone. And so a good father reflects the nature of the Cosmos by being that as well.

The other fundamental Cosmic factor underlying Fathering is the characteristics of the individual's soul, and perhaps the most crucial of these characteristics is the man's "soul age." This is the cumulative wisdom and mastery derived from the individual soul's experience.

This Quality is manifested in a "bell-shaped curve" of consciousness development in the human soul collective on this planet. The human race is just now entering into the Heart and Cosmic consciousness as a collective, though half of us have already passed that point in our development as individual souls. Now we will perforce all operate with Cosmic consciousness as our basic driving force as we pass through this Great Transition.

BIOLOGIC FACTORS

The second primary factor underlying the manifestation of Fatherhood in the human condition is our evolutionary history. The primate's social organization is a "dominance hierarchy," with an "alpha male" and his lieutenants, while the rest of the males engage in a continuous "king of the mountain" competition/combat to in effect select those who end up being able to occupy one of those positions. Meanwhile, the whole process operates as a "thrilling virility display" for the females to use as their assessment base for who will father their children.

The primary function that this social organization serves is that of protection. The male operates as the "safety perimeter," much as the musk ox form a circle around the females and the young shoulder to shoulder in the face of danger. Their strength, courage and power save the day, so to speak.

However, the fact remains that the prototypic form of all heterosexually reproducing organisms from plants on up is the female. The heterosexual system provides the needed variety of genetic material to handle the challenges of highly variegated, challenging and potentially dangerous environments.

But in order to generate that system, a sub-group of the females had to mutate into a new form that could take on the functions of protection and provision, because to do it all was too much for the female form.

The cost of this increased viability and variability was, however, that the new form of organism, called males, had to give up something like 80 degrees of the female's 360 degree capabilities to create these new capabilities in the males.

This means that Ashley Montague, a famous anthropologist was right in his book called *The Natural Superiority of Women,* because of the 280 degree males. There were several highly important capabilities that had to be "traded in" for the new competences, and males have been afraid of females ever since.

It also made the male child highly vulnerable because they have to *imprint on,* rather than to learn from their fathers. In other words, male children absorb whole processes of living from direct mimicking of their fathers which then becomes "hard wired" into their way of being.

The combination of these two "side effects" of the heterosexual viability evolution led to the primate dominance hierarchy and to the paranoid patriarchy, with all of its effects and limitations.

In particular, there are three primary resultants of this biologic history that carry over into the human condition and into fathering in a not so favorable fashion. One of these is the fiercely and sometimes even ferociously competitive, power/control/-emphasizing, dominance-seeking and combativeness propensities of the male -- especially in his "castle."

This also shows up in the "Oedipal triangle" between the 3 to 7 year of son, the father and his wife. The male is so "hard-wired" to be the ultimate authority and the king figure that he is apt to have a very difficult time not competing and combating with his son over his wife's affections.

The second biologic heritage from the primates is the intensely instrumental approach of the male. They are so task-oriented, problem-solving fixated, and results-seeking that they tend to strongly put all other considerations a long second in their priorities. They therefore tend not to be relationally, ecologically or emotionally concerned.

And the third biologic leftover is the fundamental emotional base from which males in general and fathers in particular tend to live – namely, grief. This arises out of the "buck stops here" -- "I have to do this all by myself" -- "lonely at the top" complex of the alpha male. They also tend to be commitment-avoidant, because of all the heavy and isolated responsibilities involved in their role and function.

Associated with this is the fact that the male tends to end up as the marginalized outsider figure who is distant and perhaps even excluded from the maternal/children cluster. They are both so feared and so busy doing their protection and provision things that they don't fit into the core of the community.

And this, in turn, tends to make him the unapproachable, unreachable, unavailable figure for his daughter. He is so much the "unreachable authority" and the "unattainable father" to her that she ends up in an unrequited longing position with regard to him.

ARCHETYPAL FACTORS

Archetypes are universal human experiences that functionally result in what appear to be genetically transmitted propensities, symbolisms and needs. They are powerful inherent drivers for us all.

And because of the Cosmic and biologic factors described above, there are certain Archetypal factors that operate in fathering. For one thing, the father tends to end up in the "Deity/Other" position, especially in the paranoid patriarchy that has dominated us for the last ten thousand years. They become the "absolute authority" whom women had to manipulate to get anything working and to meet any needs.

This is particularly the case for their daughter, for whom the "most rejecting parent" impact is especially potent when he is the one that usually plays that role. They then become a longing, pedastalization and self-rejection figure for her. He may also generate a "father-rescue" complex that plagues her in all manner of ways.

Fathers also become the representative of the Cosmos and the community to their child(ren), starting at about age two. They take on the value, significance, meaningfulness, generativity and contribution goal-setter and manifestation-modeling role. The son is biologically built to imprint from their father as the emulation figure in all manner of ways.

This makes the father extremely and fine-grained influential in their son's make up, personality formation, functioning and nature. It also makes it particularly devastating for the son if the father withholds validation, rejects, denigrates or refuses to mentor/model for the son. The son ends up massively self-rejecting and possibly inept and unsuccessful as a result.

These archetypal factors impact profoundly on the child in their self-manifestation, in their self-evaluation, and in their own ecological and next generation impacts. They also generate intense longings for validation from their father, and for matching the inspirational goals the father activates in his children.

In addition, the father becomes the icon of respect-ability -- or not. If not, their function devolves into how NOT to be a male/father/community and Cosmos member. They often generate distrust, disgust and rage in their child(ren), due to their violation of the Archetypical values and expectations.

That, in turn, sets off reactions like "father-fury," "authority-freak" and "tripod-rage" (the irresistible urge to kick anything with three legs). It can also generate things like "father-phobia" or "papa-pleasing." These are all crippling response patterns that permeate and undermine their child(ren)'s lives.

CULTURAL FACTORS

Unlike what is usually presented, indigenous cultures were not an idyllic simple life. It was a continuation and expansion of the primate lifestyle. They told the visiting anthropologists what was wanted to be heard.

Due to the primitivity of soul development and the primate pattern in the early days, tribal life was rather brutish and short. Things improved somewhat in the world's more tolerable ecologies during the early agricultural period, what with the domestic arts rather than the hunting arts becoming the basis for a more female-dominated pattern.

However, even that lifestyle was quite rigid and restrictive, due to the still rather primitive and strongly fear-based collective soul development level at the time. And then the female's influence was inundated by the female-phobic paranoid patriarchy that was in effect precipitated by the harsher and less hospitable and domesticity-preventing ecologies that generated much more aggressive and virulent cultures that conquered into a takeover.

From that time forward, the world culture has more or less been steamrollered by the virulence of the paranoid patriarchy in the hands of the more primitively developed males. This continued as we began moving into the third level of collective consciousness that emphasized rugged individualism, instrumentality and hierarchical dominance structures.

One of the primary resultants of this is a pronounced proclivity for the cultures of the world to be fearful of, baffled by, and hostile towards the Feminine and toward females and towards female values, priorities and wisdom. The result has been oppression, vicious violence, and the "hob-nail boot" societal structure.

More recently, there has been a trend towards the emergence of a heart-centered world, as move into the fourth level of consciousness development in our soul collective. However, this has been met with much resistance, back-sliding, and over-compensatory bellicoseness and militaristic get-backs.

It has also been a period of the "me generation," with the immaturity, selfishness, indifference, moral/ethical decline and the "don't give a damn" nihilism, cynicism and "end times" despair-rage of the boomers and the X and Y generations.

Add to that the divorce rate of 50% and climbing, 75% on second marriages, and so on, with all of the resultant effects on the children, and you have quite a difficult stew at present.

As for parenting, it has been a period of decline and fall, due to the double shifts and two worker families, the massive rise of single parent families, and the thoroughgoing neglect of children's needs in "kids come last" societies.

Indeed, there is a pronounced propensity for there to be cynical derision around the business of being involved with children and with domestic needs. This is complicated even further by the "culture of poverty," with its devastating impacts on our future adults.

There is precious little generativity (building for tomorrow) in the world culture now, and there is scarcely any teaching, modeling, honoring, exemplification, or resource-provision for parenting.

Instead, there are attacks on "welfare bilkers," removal of financial support if there is a father figure in the home, refusal of child care in the workplace, cutting back on school budgets, and in other ways a redoubling of the rejection of the Feminine -- and the Future --as a function of the "last grasp" of the dying order.

All of this has a severely negative effect on the fathering process. Indeed, it can be rather persuasively argued that there never has been any real fathering on any significant scale all the way along -- with a few extremely exceptional instances of course.

SITUATIONAL FACTORS

Here we come to the life history factors in people's experiences that produce the particular fathering patterns that are displayed. Under this general rubric are all the individual stories, as well as all the psychological and psychiatric problems and their causes.

Due to the "last grasp" and the "decline and fall of the Western Empire" process that is going on right now as we move from the old order into the new world, such personal psychopathology is extremely prevalent.

This has resulted in a rather gruesome parade of "fathering failures" in the world today. There are so many detrimental processes, forces and factors operating against the success of fathering that it is increasingly hard to find good examples of effective fathers. We now turn to these "fathering failures" that mark this point in our evolutionary process.

FATHERING FAILURE PATTERNS

One of the commonest fathering failures is the "not present." This is the workaholic, the traveler, the absentee father. But it is also the "sealed unit," the "urban hermit," the "preacher's kid," the "shrink's kid" and the "heroic," all of whom are not available for their kids. And in its most extreme form, you find the uninvolved, the withdrawn and the "non-existent."

What's involved here is that the father found out very early on that involvement was one form or another of death via the "poison apple" effect at the hands of his mother. So in effect, he has thrown in the towel on vulnerability, engagement and availability. It tends to elicit huge efforts on his kids' parts to get him to "come out." It also results in the kids' feeling it is their fault.

Next, there is the "feeling-suppressor." This is the distant, the mentalistic, the abstract academician, the non-sharer, the uncommunicative, the emotionally shut down, the totally instrumental, the computer geek, and in the worst case, the "cold one."

He found out that to be in touch with his feelings was the "kiss of death" in his family, where everybody functioned in the same manner. He in effect re-creates his home environment everywhere he goes. His effect is to frighten everyone of their feelings.

Then there is the "Peter Pan," who is childish, manipulative, explosive, convenience-concerned, and promise-breaking. He lives in the moment, and he seeks to get by on his charmingness, cunningness and cleverness, as well as on his boyish good looks. It catches up with them in middle age. They are a "Heartbreak Hotel" in their impact on their kids. It is the resultant of an over-indulging and under-requiring parenting.

Another sort of opposite pattern is the "over-responsible," who is often rather maternal in his functioning, and who can serve as the "savior figure" for one or more of his child(ren).

He tends to marry a "rejecting mother" stand-in, and he becomes the caring parent. This can even go to the extreme of his becoming the only source of love-giving, in the form of being a sexual partner with one of his kids, who then fixates on him.

He is usually taken for granted or rejected as his children focus all of their energy on trying to "get the God Housekeeping Seal of Approval" from their most rejecting parent --his wife.

Another common pattern is the "unpleasable perfectionist," for whom nothing is ever good enough. He is over-idealistic, hung up in principles, rule-bound and role-binding, judgmental, and wrong-making.

He either comes from a similar family with a father like that or he developed his pattern as a defense against a chaotic home environment. He makes people feel "bad, wrong and evil."

Another common one is the "ambulatory paranoid." These people are legalistic, secretive, rigidly conservative, and suspiciously assumptive. He can also be authoritarian, puritanical, or even militaristic in his functioning. He is the product of a similar family, as he "passes it on." They generate either complete replicas, utter rebellion or massive suppression in their child(ren).

Next, there is the "broken one" -- the weak, the non-protective, the "crushed coke can," or even the colluder with the authoritarian or crazy wife/mother. He was in effect prevented from developing himself by a virulently oppressive family. Such people generate terrible feelings of betrayal in their children.

Then there is the "severe rejecter," who constantly shames, guilt-induces and denigrates. He too is "passing it on" by doing unto others what was done unto him as a child. His effect is to be thoroughly demoralizing, debilitating and self-rejection-generating.

Still another all-too-familiar situation is the "super-selfish" pattern. Included here are the withholder, the "dead beat dad," the druggie, the drunk, the "spawn and leave," the neglectful and ignoring, the massively egocentric, self-immersed and narcissistic, and the uncaring.

But also included here is the ecologically insensitive and dominating imposer of his choices and preferences, such as the constant relocater and the ignorer of their environment and of the needs of others as he forces his lifestyle upon them.

They come from an "Everyone for themselves!" type of family environment, and they are in effect completely oblivious to their impact on others -- indeed they are uncaring about it. They are a total survivalist living in the basement of their psyche. Their impact on their children is devastating.

Another common one is the "depressive," who ends up being depleted, exhausted, amotivational, demoralized and perhaps even self-destructive or suicidal. When he is home, he is in effect a lump. He tends to elicit rescue attempts, disgust or despair in those around him. He was systematically undermined in his capacity for initiative and success.

Then there is the "fearful father." He tends to do the "Chicken Little" thing and to be avoidant and fear-contagioning in his functioning. Because of the role and impact of the father figure, this can be a fairly frightening experience for a child. He was, of course, totally terrorized by his family.

Next there is the "dependent," who turns his daughter into his mother and/or his spouse, and who has the effect of turning their relationship into a triangle with the daughter against the mother. He tends to be rescue-eliciting and "craziness of two"-generating in his impact. He was massively enmeshed and castrated by his dominatrix mother.

Of course, we can't forget the "angry father." He is aggressive and loud, or, conversely, he is a suppressed "seething volcano." In both cases, almost everything he does is in one way or another related to anger-release -- with terrible ecological effects.

If he is the aggressive type, he tends to intimidate, while if he is the seething type, he is apt to generate great fearfulness of what he might do. He is the product of an utterly enraging environment.

The next one is the "power-abuser." He takes advantage of his position/situation of being in control of the vital resources of his family to do things like manipulations, reputation-devastations, option-preventing, financial enslavement, "My rights as a father" and "For your own good" parenting, and ego-extension imposition of his uncompleted intentions onto his child(ren) to play out for him.

The "macho papa" is a variation on this theme. They are passing on their family culture extending back for generations. It has an enraging, undermining and/or demoralizing impact on his children.

And in the forefront of everybody's mind nowadays is the "sexually addicted dad" who is a womanizer and a sex-ploitater. It is due to a sexualizing mother. In its worst forms, it can go to sexual perversions, sexual abuse, and sexual assault (rape). The recipients of his functioning often feel that they somehow caused or deserved this treatment, and it can create severe self-relationship issues in his kids.

Another common pattern is the "rage-aholic," who is explosive, violent and abusive. It can go all the way out to the Neanderthal, the dangerous, and the monstrous. They are a "walking ball of rage" and an "ambulatory blast furnace." It arises out of a massively dysfunctional and explosive family. They can intimidate, drive away, or pass it on in their impact on their children.

Then there is the "disgusting father," who is incompetent, irrelevant, negatively eccentric, unadmirable, embarrassing, awkward, inept, and shame-eliciting. He is the product of a totally competence-, confidence- and success-preventing ragefully engulfing mother. He elicits rejection, rescuing or revulsion.

Next is the "cruel God" father who is vicious, malicious, sadistically passive-aggressive, virulent and crazy-making. He is on a never-ending and indiscriminate vengeance-vendetta, in a "pound of flesh for every ounce of misery" reaction to having been parented in the same manner. They are massively destructive in their impact in a variety of ways, and in the reactions they generate from their child(ren).

Of course, there is also the "psychopathic father," who is manipulative in a "gray marketer" manner as he lives out his marginal "sleazy pieces" lifestyle, such as the compulsive horse player and gambler or the con artist. Or even worse, they can get into the actively criminal and dangerous pattern. Their child(ren) usually end up going the same way or living the kind of lifestyle to which they have become accustomed.

Then there is the "jailer," who keeps his terrified family under his total domination with extreme tactics. He is a "mad king" who is massively possessive, terrorizing, gun-toting and – pointing at outsiders, insanely jealous, miserly, capricious, totally arbitrary and virulently punishing.

They can even do the "grizzly bear" thing of effectively "eating their own young" psychologically and for all intents and purposes. They are usually utterly overwhelming to their children. They come from a long string of such people.

Finally, there is the "psychotic" father -- the bizarre, distorted, and out of contact with reality individual who is manifesting a breakdown of all knowable human functioning. They quickly end up out of the family, one way or another. They are the product of a massively reality-twisting and comprehension-preventing family, usually in the presence of poor viability of their genetic structure.

EPILOGUE

That about wraps it up regarding why it is that the world is changing so rapidly, as we scuttle the paranoid patriarchy and we get on with the business of building a workable world out of the wreckage of the old order.

For there is indeed a whole new world coming, and fast. We are moving out of learning how to live in 3-D, and we are moving into continuous Cosmic contact as we learn to come from the Heart and to live in Love. That is the true nature of the present situation --the entering the next level of collective human consciousness.

One remarkable finding that is taking place nowadays is that brain scan studies are finding that adult males are transforming the operation of their brain to be like the inter-hemispheric integrating whole brain operation of the female. This is *not* developmental and it is *not* evolutionary. It is a spontaneous mutation taking place on a mass scale!

As a result of all this, there are three general groups on planet right now. One is the kind of people we have described above, who are the fully imprinted products of the old order.

The second group is composed of people who are now fully aware that we cannot, must not and will not continue the patterns of the past. Thank you, Al Gore! However, these people are also highly confused and adrift without a clear idea of what would work at present. They feel rather overwhelmed by what is happening, and they are desperately seeking solutions.

And by far the smallest group is the leadership of tomorrow, who are those old souls, who have been so far down the soul development path that they see all sides of things, and who is both tender and strong, wise and loving, inspiring and solution-generating. They are true authority figures who will lead and show the way. And, yes, half of them are males.

They model and mentor, they do it right for their girls in the Elektra and adolescent periods, and they do it right for their boys all the way along. They are the "gentle giant" fathers who are manifesting an emerging "mesh" model of inspirationally integrated, caring and competent living, sousing and fathering.

These people, working in combined forces with the "confused ones," are here to build a truly love-based world as the only viable solution to our situation. These are indeed the most interesting of times!

CHILD CARE IN THE NEW WORLD

Child care and treatment in the emerging culture is a very special process indeed. It's not uncommon to hear rueful laughter among child care people. The reason is that it is the most demanding profession in the world in many ways.

The thing about working with kids is that you are not just doing a one-on-one with a kid or even one-on-a-group. Whenever you work with a kid, you are dealing with an entire ecosystem.

You may find yourself handling a bedtime issue or a disciplinary episode or a fight-settling process or whatever. But in fact, you are really dealing with the tip of an iceberg. Any time you deal with a kid, you are dealing with that kid's entire world.

This is because they require an external support system at all times, along with an enculturation system and a protection system. And your work with them needs to be in conjunction with all of those systems.

The moment you take on a bunch of kids or even a kid, you are taking on the entire community, the society at large, and the future of the human race, along with the future of the child(ren).

We worked for ten years on the definition of what professional child care is, for legislative purposes. It is such an overwhelmingly complicated system of processes and parameters that it is almost impossible to describe measure and legislate about, much less to come up with prescriptions for professional standards.

We finally did so, and the resulting evaluation/assessment systems and definitions were incredibly subtle, complex and sophisticated. However, no sooner did we accomplish that than the world started changing so rapidly and profoundly that it became apparent that there are going to have to be continuous modifications, up-datings, contextualizing, and situational standards developed.

This is because the nature of kids and the nature of the world are evolving at such an intense pace and level that we are in effect "flying by the seat of our pants" a lot of the time as new things keep emerging on us.

The whole process got started in the mid-60s, when I was the Clinical Director of a new radical treatment agency for emotionally disturbed children. Then in 1967, everything hit the fan.

All of a sudden, the kids that were coming into the program had nothing to do with the literature on child therapy in the past has ever said. Nor did they have anything to do with the nature of the kids we had just finished designing an agency with which to treat them.

It was like the new kids were a bunch of Martians. We were thrown completely into turmoil, and the kids were tearing up the place and driving us up the skimmer handle. What was happening, of course, was that the culture was radically evolving. The 60s were upon us.

The next several years are going to be marked by much turbulence, trouble and tribulations as we are literally forced out of our selfish and destructive ways of the past via the complete disintegration of the old order to make way for a new heart-centered order in which compassion, commitment, competence, connection and contribution will rule the day.

One aspect is that the current kids are a different "breed of cat" at both the soul level and on the cultural/ego level. Though they may not experience it themselves, they are much more spiritually attuned than has ever been the case. And this is happening in a culture that is totally immersed in materialism. It's like trying to be a monk in the marketplace for them.

Their inner imperative is to manifest God's Will in the midst of a world that is quite indifferent or even hostile to such concerns as it goes into its up-against-the-wall "last grasp" intensification of the "bad old ways" in the face of the threatening requirements to radically revise who we are.

The result is a lot of disillusionment and demoralization as the children and youth can't find anything to relate to, to commit to, or to follow through on. They are then turning the situation on its head, and they are going into pointless narcissistic materialism as the only thing that they can do, with a great deal of despair and resentment underlying all this.

If you look at what we know from developmental psychology, you will find that kids today are in many ways accelerated in their developmental progression. This makes them a handful for us to deal with, because they are neither fish nor fowl, neither here nor there, and unheard of as people.

Most of the people who are rearing and those who are working with kids are finding that they have to "fly by the seat of their pants" because of the unprecedented parameters involved in the situation today.

Kids are like walking radar sets and like ambulatory alum absorbing 47 times their weight in your energy as you try to prepare them for the world of tomorrow. That's their job, and they are seeking to find out how the whole thing works.

The child caring person's job is to somehow keep sanity for themselves while at the same time giving the children as much of a reasonable representation of the realities of life and the strategies that they are going to have to utilize in dealing with life.

This is complicated by the fact that the children already know that you are in effect misrepresenting a lot of reality because of your position, situation and personality, and that you've got all kinds of big red buttons to push as they try to survive with this fool who thinks they know what they are doing with them.

The kids' experience is something like this: "I know my reality. And it ain't nothing to do with what you are telling me that reality is, all right?" And then you put them together as groups and they end up ganging up on you.

That's standard operating procedure when you are working with kids. It's the most challenging profession on the planet, especially nowadays when everything is starting to go topsy-turvy.

One of the rules of thumb that have emerged in my training of people who work with kids is that you need to know yourself and to not be freaked out by your own shortcomings. Kids are enormously tolerant as long as you are real with them. They realize what's going on because they are walking radar sets, and they are very, very sensitive.

On top of which, they've got a tremendous advantage over us called our ethical restraints and standards. They'll bop somebody on the head, yank their pants down, knock down the store display, speak the unspeakable, and run screaming from the store. And you can't do any of that.

Have you ever tried to win a control battle with a kid? Forget it! They have far more options, and those who have the most options win every time -- at least in the short run. As a result, any adult is in an automatic disadvantage with a kid in a power struggle.

Don't try it, especially if the battle of wills involves an ego trip of yours such as, "No kid is going to control ME!" or "My reputation is at stake here!" The moment the kid picks up on something like that, they are off and running.

What kids want and need is commitment. They want to know that whatever you're doing, you're doing it to the best of your ability and with the highest outcome for all in mind as the goal. They are extremely sensitive to that.

Now that doesn't mean that they don't have neuroses, or that they aren't short-sighted in their goals, or that they don't have temper tantrums over broccoli. But it *is* true that in the long run and for the large part, they are extremely attuned to reality.

Kids in treatment programs especially are aware at some level of the trials and tasks facing them, and of the unprecedented challenges they are going to have to deal with. Indeed, because of all that, they are particularly demanding of whatever we can provide for them in the way of honest and relevant preparation.

On the other hand, I must say at this juncture that there are a bunch of kids who are here on planet to experience "the last train to Clarksville." We are coming to the end of strictly biological evolution via the "Armageddon" process.

And the "Clarksville" people are the "crash and burn crew" who are here to experience the last chance to learn from "life in the fast lane" on that "last train." When this era is over, there will be no more opportunities to live in a world that is dominated by evil. And the kids in this group show all the characteristics of the past patterns of the human race. These are in effect the "all the king's horses" people.

In the future, after the transition crisis process, we will have shifted from a negativity-minimizing to a positivity-maximizing motivational and operational system. This is the most momentous era in human history. It is time for us to "make it or break it" as a collective soul pool. Either we get it together or we get out.

And all the indications are that we have reached the "tipping point" on this, and that after the transition/transformation crunch period, we will be working from the upper three chakras -- the loving Heart, the wise Throat, and the spiritually integrating Third Eye, rather than from the first chakra physical survival, the second chakra emotional survival, and the third chakra social/ecological survival.

Our earlier evolutionary process was one of overcoming the density pull of evil, which is "live" spelled backwards via violating the physical, emotional and bio-social laws of the Cosmos.

We are about to move from survival mentality to universal Love and unlimited Energy. We will be going for broke in our attempt to build a world that is based on compassion, commitment, competence, connection and contribution.

For the non-"crash and burn" kids, this means that they have a very high probability of being thrust into positions of considerable responsibility early in their lives, due to the circumstances of these times. And they need training in how to integrate spirituality and practicality on the every-day level.

These kids are facing something like a quadruple challenge process. First they are connecting with spirituality in their inner being in a manner not seen on a mass level before. Second, they have an aura about them that makes them seem deviant.

Then there is the "marginal man" felt alienation from the world where they are neither fish nor fowl. And finally, they are aware at some level of the profundity of the situation we are all facing, and of their central role and responsibility in it.

The situation today is that we have more than half of the population in the lower levels of consciousness who are in effect bringing down the old order by so pushing the limits of the former way of being in a manner that removes the systems that would destroy the human race and the planet.

They are doing it by not caring about their responsibilities and their ecological impact by living out of intense selfishness, like the assembly line worker who is callously careless in what they are doing on the line and the corrupt corporations and politicians greedily lining their pockets while destroying the economic and moral infrastructure of society.

That type of disintegration is setting the stage for a major crisis arising from the ecological habitat deterioration and from the cumulative effects of all the selfishness, irresponsibility, asininities and the various and sundry other "monkey wrenches in the works."

The other function the "crash and burn crew" will serve is to leave the planet in droves by all manner of means, with the largest being a wave of plagues. This will remove the primitive consciousness and the "evil" people, leaving only those who are operating from the Heart chakra and higher on the planet.

What this will do is to thrust those who are coming from the upper chakras into pivotal positions of influence and responsibility as a function of their efficaciousness and because of their values in action as inspirational role models.

Our job is to basically start elevating the consciousness of the human race as our top priority process. And that requires that we clear out our neuroses and those of the kids now. In other words, "Know thyself, don't be ashamed of yourself, and don't be defensive of yourself" as you focus on your contribution, especially as we work with the kids.

Kids are aware when you are working with them. These kids are tuned into all this stuff. That's why working with them is such an unusual experience nowadays -- they are an extraordinary batch of people.

They are an odd amalgamation of the normal biologic being called "children" while at the same time being the leaders of tomorrow in these extraordinary times. And they are going to do it much sooner and more rapidly than the usual developmental process would lead you expect to have happen. The process is inevitable, the stakes are enormous, and working with these kids therefore goes way beyond that which has heretofore been required of us.

Those who work with these kids should have a healthy self-respect for what they are doing. They have to basically pioneer processes that not even professional child therapists have had to deal with in the past.

It requires tremendous capability and commitment to pull this off. This is why we find ourselves wiped out at the end of the day. It is almost overwhelming, but it is also extraordinarily important. These kids are the world of tomorrow and beyond.

In addition, there is a tremendous acceleration of change as we approach the critical mass point. There are two things going on at once in this process. One is the decline and fall of the Western Empire. The other is the emergence of the Heart Chakra as our base of operations. And in both, we have reached the point of no return.

The world we grew up in and that the human race evolved in is gone forever. This means that we are going to have to go through some pretty mind-warping changes, and we are going to have to generate kids who can face a world that is radically different.

Now all parents today were raised in the old order, and we are still stuck in it at the present time. As a result, most parents are doing their best to keep up with the enormous changes that are being demanded of them. At the same time, they have to dig out from the mess that was created in their heads by the way the past was.

But it is still inevitable that you are going to have to build a culture with the kids you work with that is radically different from their family culture. And in this era, this is a particularly difficult problem.

One aspect of this is that re-entry into family and society by children who have had to be treated away from home is a monumental process because the kids have to somehow transfer what they are learning in the agency to their family, and their family has to adapt to their new child who is preparing to handle the world of tomorrow.

I once took a training in which the fundamental rule was, "No Helping!" This is quite a situation when the room suddenly becomes 165 people of different sizes. I watched a 6 year old woman work out a sophisticated self-commitment contract with no help from anyone.

What those two words did was to blow the kids' covers, and they dropped their "child" role and the roles they played in their families as they started showing who they really were.

The reality is that children aren't "children" -- they are people with souls. They are also biologically immature, uninformed and likely to get completely out of hand, due to the potency of their souls and their lack of awareness of what life requires. In this, they are in effect ALL indigos and crystal children, really.

So you have to work with them at both levels at once, with an eye to helping them cope with the world as it is, and to take on the world of tomorrow when they have to. On the other hand, kids are remarkably resilient. They will adjust and they will forgive almost anything, so long as it doesn't irreparably damage them.

And with regard to the re-entry from a treatment agency problem, a useful technology is to start some pre-agency departure rehearsal role-plays and discussions, so as to get them thinking about what it's going to be like to go back to their family, to the public school, and to whatever else they are returning to.

The other thing this sort of process does is to teach them how to go about developing strategies for transitioning from one culture to another. Which is what they are going to have to be expert at, because as the leaders of tomorrow, they are going to have to deal with people that they have to bring along into the new world.

One of the primary parameters of anyone's life is what is called the "age cohort." That refers to when they were born in terms of the world culture they were imprinted on. Such age cohorts used to be what was called a "generation" -- thirty three years from the time a person joined the "command generation" at age 30 till the point where they started to prepare to retire at age 63.

Now the world is changing so fast that the age cohort is about 3 years long. For instance, the first Kennedy assassination impacted a 6 year old very differently from the impact it had on a 3 year old at the time.

The 6 year old had twice as much life experience and personality evolution, and their brain had made the change from early childhood to middle childhood. As a result, the meaning of things was larger to them than they were to the 3 year old.

Now the 6 year old knew that "Big Daddy" had been malevolently killed suddenly, with all the implications of that, at least at the emotional gut-get level. Meanwhile, the 3 year old was wondering what all the fuss was about. All they knew was that everybody was extremely upset, and that scared the hell out of them.

Now that difference of Kennedy 1 between the two children made an enormous difference in their life from then on. The 6 year old started living in a world in which evil wins, the rug can be yanked at any time, hope for the old order was over for good, etc.

Meanwhile, the 3 year old just went through a temporary upheaval, and they subsequently took for granted what the old order was on its way out, that we have to build a new one as we go, and that there ARE no "Big Daddy's" to depend on, period.

This raises the question of how much kids of different ages can handle and about what kind of a world they have lived in with regard to what kinds of information is to be presented to them, in what manner, and with what context of meaning for them.

So within those constraints, you basically try to be as out-front and real as you can be with kids, because they need to know within the limits of what they can assimilate. They need all the truth they can get to deal with the confusing world. And the role of the age cohort with regard to the impact and implications of the big cultural events is a major consideration in working with them.

On top of which, the moment a kid spots somebody being phony, they go for the jugular. They hate being lied to or withheld from on crucial matters because their life depends on being able to count on the adults around them.

And that is particularly true nowadays, because of all the issues and processes that we are discussing here. They are preparing to build a world that is coming from the Heart Chakra, in which Cosmic correctness will have to be manifested in all we do -- in every Institution we create, in every product we make, and in every service we deliver.

The kids today know that they basically have to deal with totally new events, requirements and parameters in a highly unpredictable world. They realize that they are going to have to carve out a whole new reality by the seat of their pants for the rest of their life.

If you lie to them, you are going to have to pay the price. So if you are in over your head with them, gently let them know that, and elicit their assistance in the process of figuring out what is the better way to do things.

It's very easy to get into fearfulness, guilt-wilt, or a power-mongering ego trip with them. You have to re-think whatever you consider kids to be, to know that the buck stops with you so that you have to make all kinds of decisions, and to know that you have to handle all the stuff of life with them.

But the moment you get into one of these ego trips, the kid knows it's a "Lord of Flies" situation in which the most primitive and coercive people will rule the roost. That scares them, and consequently they'll go bananas on you.

They'll do whatever it takes to get you back in the driver's seat in a reasonable, truly relevant, sensible and sensitive manner. They'll go to any extremes of options to get you to come through for them.

When one of these challenging things comes down, you simply have to shrug your shoulders, pick up the pieces, make lemonade out of the situation, and learn from it. That is the best way to approach the whole kit and kaboodle.

The kids are starting to pioneer some of the new world forms in their funny little ways, within their biologic limitations as immature human beings. Because of their peculiar situation and the nature of the world at large, they are teaching the adults around them right now.

Working with them can be tough, demanding, overwhelming, exhausting, irritating, frustrating, alarming, and sometimes depressing. Nonetheless, it will leave you tremendously expanded, and it is an irreplaceable opportunity.

The key to working with them is to *respect* them -- immaturity, limitations, role play-outs and all. And you have to be juggling your own issues with them all the time, of course. Things like your own unresolved childhood traumas, the "you can't do unto others what was done unto you" phenomenon, you're feeling in over your head, your pet peeves, your just wanting to have a good time with them, your responsibility-deflecting, your blind-spots, your skill holes, etc.

You simply have to come to terms with the fact that these kids are bottom line souls, and at the same time, you are dealing with the fact that they just punched somebody out and they are saying, "He did it! It's his fault!"

The fact of the matter is that you are providing them with unique experiences that are extremely powerful and important in their lives and therefore in the world of tomorrow. In these times, these kids are relying on you to do the best you can to provide them with some kinds of guidelines, assistance and development-engendering for meeting the demands of their lives.

While it is true that you often feel like you are flying by the seat of your pants, over your head, pissed off at the kids or the world, and not knowing what you are doing with them, nevertheless, if you are basically aware of and accountable for who you are and you don't let your ego get in the way when you work with them, they'll go the whole nine yards with you. And all of you will come out of the whole experience with remarkably expanded souls.

As for working with parents, that has to be done on the basis of your best judgment calls. Every parent's situation is different, and you have to remember that *their* parents are also a key part of the kids' ecology.

And in turn, the parents are a part of a larger ecology to which they have to respond. The issue of child confidentiality on the one hand, and of parent-assistance and compassionate comprehension on the other, with regard to what you should share about what you have learned with and about the kid is a tricky issue.

You never know what to say to the parents with any confidence, because you never know what kind of bomb you might be dropping or what they kids have done with the "Mommy, so-and-so said . . ." phenomenon.

And like with the kids quoting you, there is the problem of "mis-contexting" -- the parent(s) taking something out of mid-sentence or out of the midst of a whole complex situation and dropping it into another situation in a manner that makes you sound like you are the world's worst "moral cretin" or that you are giving the parents justifications for doing dastardly deeds to the kids.

The best strategy seems to be "discretion is the better part of disclosure." Most parents have not had the kind of expanding experiences that their kids and you have had. As a result, what seems like a perfectly common sense everyday knowledge about kids and about reality is *not* common sense reality to them because they haven't been there.

The fact is that anyone who works with kids has to deal with the entire community sooner or later, because kids require all those support systems and because they affect so many systems.

All those systems feel that they have a priority claim on these kids with regard to knowledge about them, control of them, their importance in the system's functions, what's going on, etc.

So any time you disclose anything about a kid or from a kid to any part of the kid's ecological system, you have to be thinking about what is the nature and role of that system in the child's life and vice versa. It's better not said if you suspect you're going to say something that is going to potentially cause harm.

One thing to remember in all this is that the kid's soul chose to have those parents for purposes of its own that we can't know. The kid will blow the cover on any negative situation when they are finished learning from it, unless the situation is so overwhelmingly dangerous that they can't do that. And then that itself is a soul-designed destiny decision.

Or we may be dealing with a "last train to Clarksville" kid who needs to have a downhill descent for their soul-expansion. For instance, when you have a child in a family that is engaging in subtle and sly sadism or a gradual destruction process towards the kid, it is usually better to be discreet than to try to blow the cover on the scene because of all the kickback effects, especially on the kid.

This usually leads to all sorts of mayhem reaction effects that do the child no good. Everything you say will be used against you and the kid in ways you never dreamed of because you have stuck your oar into a whirlpool of expert disaster-generators.

Another aspect of the situation is the child him/herself. You need to do an accurate assessment of who they are to the best of your ability, so that you have some idea of what and how they will disclose to the parents and other members of their ecology.

You might decide to try to work with the kid to develop their own self-protection systems. But at the same time, you don't want to put the kid into a control battle with their parents. So you discuss the situation with the kid in the most strategic manner possible.

For instance, suppose you have been informed by a qualified professional that the child's diet is in effect poisoning them. You might conduct a life space interview with the child that looks something like the following. "Well, what's it like about that food business at home? What do you think would happen if we or you tried to change your diet at home?"

You just sort of explore with them, and you try to get some notion of how much the kid or you can influence their food intake, and how much the kid is willing to do and why. Also, check out how gamy their family is likely to be, because very often kids with families like this are just as dangerous as the parents are. You basically do the best you can with what you've got and with what the situation is.

One of the real dangers and dilemmas in child care or therapy is the risk of going down the tubes with the kid. There are so many situations where you can't do anything about it, and the danger is of becoming so despairing about what you are experiencing and your inability to make a difference that you are in danger of falling into a depressive spiral.

You have to develop what I call "protective apathy." After you've done an ethical job of assessment of the whole set of circumstances as far as you can ascertain and obtain and you find that you are not in a position to make any impact on the situation, and then you go into protective apathy, rather than to engage in a kamikaze attack or a despair freak-out.

Because if you don't use protective apathy and you go down the tubes, the world loses a valuable resource for tomorrow, and for what? This is just a part of the business of working with children.

The kid is just the tip of the iceberg. The rest of the iceberg has control over the kid's environment and circumstances, and ninety-nine percent of the people who have that control have no concept or even one tenth of what you know about who about who the kid is. And they don't know that they don't know or even worse, they don't *want* the kid to get better.

Welcome to the world of child care and treatment. But remember, the kid's soul knows what it is doing with all this. And then there is the occasional parent who knows more than you do about the kid and who is quite sophisticated spiritually, so that they are a major asset in the situation-improvement process.

So you assess the situation as best you can, and you use the "discretion is the better part of disclosure" criterion. You also use the "match and lead" process, whereby you check out where the people are at, and you make your moves congruent with the family's circumstantial and psychological space.

And then you gradually bring them along to a better match to the realities of their situation and the kid's needs in keeping with their pace of being able to move along. So you start where they are and gently bring them to where you are and where the kid's needs are.

See if you can match up with the family's pattern of behavior, their value system and their manner of talking in the way that you approach them. Then you drop in a few extras that are one step ahead of where they were before that they might be able to buy into. And by degrees, you move them closer to a match with their kid's needs.

If you come in and "blow the Emperor's cover" you know what he's likely to do to the little boy who did that to him (namely you). So seek to make your intervention fit in with where the Emperor is at and build from there.

Another theme that comes up when working with children is the role of their need for structure. You are dealing with individuals who are biologically speaking not yet sophisticated enough to run their own mind on things completely.

So what you do is to set up a cage, and then within that cage you set up as much of a democratic and free will process as you can. The amount of latitude that the situation is given is based on the child's degree of demonstrated responsibility that they put out.

That's a constantly negotiated thing, and the more that you get the kids involved in the process for learning purposes the better. Set them up with committees of five kids to help each other run their show if you can. Start teaching them self-government and self regulation. But at the same time, you have to have firm outer limits.

On the other hand, that doesn't mean that you set up a total external control system or an authoritarian process. You try to set up as much structure as they need and no more or less.

You basically allow them to earn their way into more latitudes, and it is often very useful to have a series of latitude steps formally laid out so they can work their way up the ladder of self-responsibility and privilege.

They need behavioral criteria and sequences of disciplines in terms of what happens if they blow it, along with a process of determining who sets up the nature of the situation, etc. Working with kids requires a lot of structure. It also requires a lot of flexibility, compassion and ingenuity.

You start with an initial structure of your best design, and then you wait for feedback from the events that transpire. Inevitably there will be mistakes -- you were too restrictive or you were too loose and lax in the latitude you set up. The sequence of events, the kids, and the other staff will give you the feedback you need.

So you sit down and re-negotiate the structure with them. That is a very valuable experience for kids. They've already experienced that the first system didn't work. So they will be very involved in helping set up a second system that hopefully does work.

They know better than you do that they need structure, but they also know that they don't want bull. So you work with them the best that you can to set up the sanest and growth-expanding structure that you can. You start by setting up an arbitrary system so they have something besides a "Lord of the Flies" situation to enter. And then you co build with them from there.

You might even say, "Well, we're going to do this for a week, kids." These are the rules for this week. At the end of this week, we're going to sit down and see where we're at. And don't try to pull any fast ones on me because I know what I'm doing and so to the rest of us.

On the other hand, we're going to listen to you because you've got information and experiences to share with us that are important. And we will work out to the best of our abilities a structure that we can all agree upon.

"So be thinking about it, because what we decide at the end of this week lasts for the time that we are here." And of course, that is subject to the vicissitudes of life that require even later revisions of the system, but it gets the message across.

As we move into the new world, the kids will probably require even tighter structure in some ways because of the increasing uncertainty out there, and because of their brilliant capabilities for getting into trouble.

But again, you have to do your best at reading everything and at working things out as well as you can within the context of the situation, drawing upon right knowledge of the parameters, personalities, souls and destinies involved. There are no hard and fast rules for this type of thing. You have to basically try for the best you can get going to make it all work.

One interesting model is to set up schools where the parents assist in the teaching -- parents as teachers. It's done on a volunteer basis with screening, with a strong cultural expectation of participation and contribution, but with awareness that some parents are simply not suited to teach or child care. There also need to be other volunteer jobs that parents can do, so that everyone does their part.

In such a program, the parents do a certain number of hours per week in the agency. You work out the best you can with the circumstances you are faced with at any given point in time with regard to the what the situation is, who the parents are, what the staff situation is, etc.

Then there's politics, personalities and policies. These are "nasty words," but they are a necessary component of any program as far as the way things can be allowed to work. Sometimes the politics, personalities and policies aren't the greatest, but setting the ground work on which everything else has to be founded simply has to be done.

If it is found that these factors are strangling the agency, it's time to sit down and revise the rules and roles so as o make what the kids and everyone else is experiencing the best it can be, given the resources available and the situation at hand.

There are no set answers to this kind of stuff. It's basically a continuous assessment and problem-solving system. That's why child care and therapy is so incredibly complex, competence-demanding and abilities-expanding.

It requires so much of you around so many areas with regard to issues of such importance. It is the most challenging, rewarding and significant system that you can get involved in. It really pays off, but it is also really hard work.

The general idea is to start with you running the show and with its ultimately ending up with the children largely running it. For instance, there's the resource called the "Magic Circle." This involves daily sitting down with all the kids and all the staff at the beginning of the day and tuning into each other, problem-solving, planning and preparing for the day.

It's like a house-meeting for the kids. You model for them how to go about the handling of personalities, policies, pragmatics, politics and priorities. You teach spiritual and ethical principles, practical survival skills, and the like with all that happens.

As much as possible, get the kids involved in whatever it is that you are doing with the agency. The kids need that kind of responsibility training, and they need help in the development of it.

If you set it up as an "us against them" kind of thing, you are going to be over-run and outclassed from the very beginning. But if you set it up as a "win-win for us" thing, it makes all the difference in the world.

However, at the same time, we need to take into account the pragmatic realities of the fact that these kids have not been around long enough to have certain equipment and experience.

Some are more advanced, and some are behind, and you take these differences into account as you are working. And you help the kids take those things into account so that they can learn to do that in a spiritually enlightened and uplifting manner.

One final comment. At times when working with kids, you have to enforce a rule or a process that is allowed or that is denied in the world at large. The kids then object on the basis of what is acceptable in the community.

The best response to that is to say something like, "Look, you're in this place and in here, soda pop, comic books and candy don't cut it, and for very good reasons." They'll get that and understand it. The general idea is to be real and yet to provide the structure and the experiences that they need. They know in their hearts that your heart is in it then.

As was said in the beginning, child care and treatment in the new world is a very special process indeed. It takes everything you have and then some, it stands your hair on end, it drives you to distraction, but it is also a true bliss experience in many ways. As was said, they teach their parents (and you) well, and they are bringing you along with them into the heart-centered new world.

The INDIGOS And The CRYSTAL CHILDREN

There is in effect a Cosmic level revolution going on under our very noses. What is happening is the joining of the human soul pool by two other soul pools, meaning that we have human bodies occupied by three different soul pools now.

One of them is called the "indigos" because of the color of their aura. Their aura has no orange, yellow, green or blue in it. There is the red of the first "survival" chakra at the base of their spine and the violet of the "hot line" to the "Home Office" (All That Is) at the seventh or crown chakra. But in between is the color of the sixth or "third eye" chakra, and the sixth chakra runs their show.

They have been gradually coming in over about a century, but with a very sharp increase over the last thirty years. The other new soul pool is called the "crystal children" and they have been increasingly coming in over the last ten years.

Both are highly etherial and upper chakras in their base of operations. The human soul pool is on the average based around the top of the third chakra and going into the fourth chakra. These new soul pools are coming in to elevate the consciousness of the human biological form.

The collective destiny of the human race is moving into the "sacred teacher" function at this time. Our ultimate destiny is to disseminate all three soul pools out into the universe to guide the development of all souls in this universe through the spiritual/Cosmic manifestation process.

Both new soul pools are in effect Cosmic Einstein's, and they know their past lives and their destiny consciously, at one level or another. Now human souls also know these things, but at least thus far, our in-body egos haven't.

The other characteristic of both entering soul pools is that they are *all* old souls. This is a gigantic soul evolutionary leap forward for the human race, and it has huge implications.

Both incoming groups can read auras (the state of someone's emotional body), the mind (the state of the mental body), past lives, and destinies. They are here to encompass us, to understand who we are and what we are undergoing.

They are movers and shakers, innovators and transformers, leaders and guides. They can draw upon their soul experience to generate new resources, concepts, patterns and directions of development.

However, they are not "overlords" or "grounded gods." They are much more evolved and experienced than we are in the upper chakras. But we are more experienced in the lower chakras -- in the workings of 3-D. Our future relationship with them will be co-creative, with each drawing upon their own strengths and learning from the other new pool and from us.

Now the vast majority of these two new soul pools are occupying what are children's bodies because they have to go through the developmental process to be able to work with human bodies on this planet.

That generates a rather interesting phenomenon. Which is one minute they will fix their ages-old wisdom upon you and you do what you can to tap into your soul to meet them half way.

And then, true to their being kids, they'll be throwing a temper tantrum over broccoli, and you have to use all the traditional child-rearing techniques like the time-out chair to teach their egos how to function effectively here.

And the ironic thing about this "alternating current" process is that their soul part is fully aware of what they need, and they are totally appreciative of their getting the training when their biologically immature part is receiving those experiences. They *know* they need to learn how to handing 3-D.

The phenomenon is a literal show-stopper. Consider the problem of a baby soul adult in a baby soul culture like the Middle East having to handle all these much older soul Cosmic Einstein's in their midst.

It is for this reason that he authors of the first major book on the indigos have been called before the United Nations several times. Incidentally, as of fall of 2000, there were 49,000 entries on the indigos alone on the internet.

I have described the situation of a lot of indigos when the large gap between who they are and what we do with them, which is unfortunately all too often not give them what they need.

Which is the Big Three -- Love, Relevance and Respect. They tend to become rather intensely agitated, resentful, disgusted and disruptive because of that. They cannot and will not tolerate being deprived of these three fundamental experiences. The following is a kind of syndrome description of what happens to them under these circumstances that I wrote up.

"Super-being misfit." They are an "advance guard" person who is focused on etheric and spiritual patterns, phenomena and processes. They are therefore an intuitive and an empath claire-sentient who is a kinesthetic and tactile learner.

They don't learn well from visual or auditory inputs alone. They need to handle something when they are learning, and they also need to be touched when spoken to, so as to "ground" them into what is being communicated.

They are highly feeling-oriented, emotional and physical, and they become bored and restless when they don't get the kind of stimulation they need. They are right-brain-dominated, but they tend to be something of a "control-freak."

This is due to the overwhelm reaction they often experience in our predominantly visual/auditory world. They feel "alone and alien" a lot of the time, and they are prone to become non-compliant, because of their pronounced sense of being "different."

It also arises from their sense of the irrelevance of much more of what goes on around them. They need caring, respectful, creative and above all relevant dialogue from their surrounding ecology.

And what they get instead is all too often Ritalin (an amphetamine), subjected to mental health system interventions, and all manner of other grossly wrong "treatments." They are often diagnosed with Attention Deficit Disorder (ADD), with or without Hyperactivity.

There were two such individuals whose parents were "benignly neglectful" -- so involved in their own world that they were not there for these boys. For that reason, they did not even notice for three months that the boys were building bombs in the garage. I am referring to the Columbine boys, of course.

Now that was an extreme case scenario as a cosmic intervention with us to get us to "wake up and smell the coffee." Of course, the initial reaction was a gun control panic, but over time, we have become increasingly aware that there is something drastically wrong with what we are doing with our children. This was the object lesson of the event for us.

We simply MUST rise to this challenge. It is our future and the future of our children that is at stake here. We have to re-think and re-tool everything to meet the nature of the new human race that is appearing in our midst world-wide. We are being required by these incoming guides to evolve NOW.

WHO *ARE* THE INDIGOS?

There is a great deal that we don't know about these new people. We will have to learn as we go in this process. However, there are some characteristics of the indigos that have been discovered thus far. This section deals with these preliminary findings.

The indigo is an individual who approaches everything from the vantage point of what could be characterized as "third eye" understanding. The "third eye" mind is the sacred/secular integrator and interpreter. It also integrates the processes and outcomes of the left hemisphere, the right hemisphere, the body's manifestations, the world at large, and the Cosmos.

They pull everything together with everything else, and they have a comprehensive comprehension and a sacred/secular integrative Cosmic understanding of everything. They can put the most disparate things together and make sense of it from a Cosmic perspective. They are aware of the Cosmic implications, ramifications and indications of things.

And so what happens is that these people have a pair of eyes that look like Cosmic X-ray machines, with the result that they have the effect of staring you into the floor with this life energy intensity ad their penetrating perceptivity. What people get is this "nail me to the wall" and "seeing right through me" pair of eyes looking at them.

Indigos are primarily the "Cosmic consultant" and the sacredly inspired guide whose job it is to educate and elevate consciousness. They tend to be somewhat sealed off from society because of their function, and because their wisdom and intensity are often rather alarming to others.

They therefore tend to also be rather apprehensive at some level about what might happen to them at the hands of other people. As a result, they are apt to be a self-protective loner-outsider and an isolated eccentric to one degree or another.

However, due to the great changes that are taking place at present, there is now a rather radical shift in their role in the world. They are now being desperately needed to re-dress the balance and to bring Cosmic wisdom and comprehensive comprehension to bear on the situation at hand at every level of society and in every occupational undertaking. They are still having difficulty fitting in, but we need them very badly now and things will improve for them a great deal soon.

Yet at the same time, they need us because of our profound practical wisdom arising from our evolutionary process on this planet. They need "grounding" in the realities of 3-D functioning and in the space/time world.

We are all-too-well-experienced in how difficult that is. At the same time, we have learned enough from the "School of Hard Knocks" with Evil and the Headmaster ("evil" being "live" spelled backwards -- learning from our mistakes) that we can now join with them to co-create a whole new level of manifestation in the world.

The "CRYSTAL CHILDREN"

The other new wave of children coming in started about the year 2000. They are the next step in human evolution. Their function is to teach us about our inner potency and divinity. They live in the Law of One in Unity Consciousness, and they are a profound force of Love and Peace, as they are in effect "human angels."

That is, they are a new soul pool that is joining the indigo children and the human soul pool in taking on the task of developing the next step in the nature and manifestation of the human potential.

The most notable thing about them is their eyes, which are large, penetrating, hypnotic and telepathic. Their aura is opalescent, like pastel mother-of-pearl. Their speech development is often delayed until about age 3 or 4. In the interim, they combine mind-to-mind communication, self-developed sign language, and various sounds, including music, in their interactions with others.

They are intensely caring, communicative and cuddly, and at the same time, they are quite philosophical and spiritually gifted in a kind and sensitive manner. They come from the sixth dimension of consciousness, with the ability to develop to the Christ consciousness level and beyond. They can not only read our minds, they can know what is in our hearts.

They are intensely sensitive to all vibrational input, such as magnetic, electromagnetic, environmental, electrical, aromatic, aural, color and all other vibrational frequencies, and they tend to have real difficulty dealing with things and people that are not at their higher vibrational and dimensional sensitivity level. They also tend to blow out electric and electronic equipment as they adjust to being on this plane.

They are highly creative and potent, and they have no time for fear and victim dramas. They are very aware of the importance of being well-grounded in material reality, and of not getting lost in some vaguely etherial paradisiacal plane.

Nevertheless, they do have multi-dimensional awareness, and they play with spiritual development in a magical and blessed manner as they prepare to take full stewardship of the planet along with the indigos and us.

We are presently carbon-based beings, but we are transitioning into the only other four-pointed atom, silicone, in the crystalline form, like diamonds. They are here to take us all into continuous awareness of the interconnectedness of everything, and into the higher dimensions, as we leave biologic form and we enter our light bodies only wearing our bodies as "uniforms" like in the film, "Cocoon."

PROBLEMATIC PARENTING PATTERNS DICTIONARY

This is a succinct review of the ways in which the isolation of the nuclear family in the context of the paranoid patriarchy, the materialistic society, the "kids come last" value system, and the cultural implosion in transition to the new world have led to the substantial breakdown of the parenting process.

It is due to the fact that kids' needs are not being met in a large way. Children are regarded as the "proletariat" who has to be indoctrinated into the values of the soulless corporate culture and the corrupt government of today.

In addition, the needs of the isolated nuclear family couple are also relegated to the bottom of the hierarchy of priorities in the world at this time. This means that the parenting process has to be sandwiched between the requirements of survival and of succeeding in the surrounding society.

The net effect is, it is virtually inevitable for parenting failure patterns to emerge ubiquitously in the current scene. Part of these breakdowns of optimal parenting come from the neurotic patterns induced by *our* parents' own up-bringing, and part of them come from the completely dominant anti-parenting priorities of the surrounding environment.

What follows is a catalogue of a good number of such parenting pattern failures. They are not meant to be pejorative to the parents, though sometimes that is the only real way to respond to how the parents are mishandling their children, due to their catastrophic parenting.

For the most part, these problematic parenting patterns arise as a function of the fact that no one's needs are being truly met at the present time. It is for this reason that there is a gigantic upheaval and evolutionary process under way to bring about a sensible society in which the needs of families are at the top of the priority list, in recognition that nothing less than our continued existence as a species and as a planet are at stake.

Some of the items will have underlining. These are official psychiatric diagnostic categories. Others will have quotes around them. These are actual patterns that are known, but for which there are no psychiatric categories. And some will not have quotes or underlings. These are informal psychiatric terms, older diagnostic categories or disorders under consideration for becoming an official diagnosis.

With this short introduction, we turn to the ways in which the world has forced us all to malfunction in the all-important undertaking called parenting.

"ABANDOING" PARENT (1)

"Doing unto others." They are incapable of commitment and connection, due to the fact that they have never experienced it coming their way from the very beginning. They are a self-made person who had to go it alone, and they are setting up their child(ren) to do the same.

"ABANDONING" PARENT (2)

"Jumping ship." They feel that they are in way over their head, and they are leaving the scene. They are incapable of the depth of commitment and responsibility that child-rearing requires, because they never received any real child-rearing themselves.

"ABANDONMENT-THREATENING" PARENTING PATTERN

"If you do . . ." They use the notion that they will leave their child(ren) on a desert island in order to control them. It arises from having been placed on a strongly contingent love basis as a child.

"ABUSIVE" PARENTING PATTERN

"Passing it on." They have very poor frustration-tolerance and ability to empathize or comprehend others' experiences and needs. They therefore become intensely infinitely aggressive when demanded of or needed from. And, of course, this profoundly impacts on their child(ren) in a "passing it on" manner.

They were subjected to the same treatment as a child.
****

"Just desserts." They are engaged in self-rejection and self-hatred generating "deserved punishment" behaviors that arose beyond the initial period of the severe abuse at the hands of their parent(s). The parent is reacting to projected self-hatred through their identification with their child(ren).

They are also doing unto others what was done to them. They have no ability to give love, having never had it themselves.
****

"Vengeance-vendetta." They are taking it out on their child(ren), as they do unto others what was done to them in their sadistic, vengeful and cruel family.

EMOTIONAL ABUSE

"Hurting back." They are taking all their rage and pain out on their helpless child(ren). They are avenging themselves indirectly through their child(ren). They were subjected to similar treatment as a child, and they were unable to do anything about it. Now they can, and they are.

FINANCIAL ABUSE (Withholding financial resources deprivingly)

"Oh no you don't!" They are taking advantage of their position to subject their child(ren) to the type of deprivation and degradation that they experienced as a child.

PHYSICAL ABUSE

"Passing it on." The parent(s)' general orientation is that, it is the only thing that works, or all that they can do on the one hand, or that it worked for them and for generations back and for everyone else, on the other.

In these cases, the "chain of pathology" continues.
****

"Just desserts." They are caught up in self-rejection and self-hatred generating "deserved punishment" behaviors (beyond the initial period of the abuse). The perpetrator is reacting to projected self-hatred through identification with their child(ren).

They are also doing unto others what was done unto them. They have no ability to give love, having never had it themselves.
****

"Running amok." They routinely regress to extremely primitive functioning, due to very poor frustration-tolerance and coping skills. They are having "lose it" -- "blind rage" episodes in which they operate like a decerebrated (cortex removed) animal.

They were prevented from developing effective functioning in their severely dysfunctional and primitive family system.
****

"Systematic cruelty." They are sadistically inclined in all their interpersonal relationships, but especially with the powerless. They were subjected to the same treatment as a child, and it became their role model and sole manner of functioning.

POWER ABUSE

"Authoritarian asshole." Power is the name of the game for them, and nothing else matters to them. It is a pattern being passed on from their family.

SEXUAL ABUSE

"Misguided love." They are highly primitive in their emotional development, and they act out sexually towards those they feel love towards. They mean well, but they are severely inappropriate in their love expression with their child(ren).

They are the product of a maturity-undermining and severely dysfunctional family.
****

"Playing doctor." They are in effect an emotional peer of their child(ren), and they are in effect playing with them and/or expressing their affection in a highly inappropriate manner.

They are an emotional child who never got past middle childhood in their development due to severely invasive mothering. At times, this can be a very loving but hopelessly inadequate parenting situation.

They were systematically undermined and infantilized as a child, and they have in effect never gotten out of childhood.
****

"Desperately seeking Susan." They are putting the child(ren) in their parent/God/ spouse position in an emotional starvation and worth-deprivation reaction. They are trying to heal the devastating impact of severe maternal deprivation, followed by paternal rejection.
****

"I can't stop myself!" They become "possessed" in either a dissociative and/or an overwhelmingly motivated manner. It is a pattern that got started in their severely sex-ploitive, denial-dominated, suppressive and dysfunctional family.
****

"It's my right!" They are doing unto others what was done to them, either helplessly as their own pathology takes over or collusively or even proudly, as they manifest their own pathology and devastating history.
****

97

"Raging rapist." They have a vengeance/power-tripping mentality in which they are acting out their profound frustration over their effective powerlessness by "lording it over" their child(ren).

It is the result of being treated as "special" by a sex-ploitive mother to such a degree that they are in effect derailed from their destiny, and they are out for revenge.
****

"Doing unto others." They are on a sadistic vengeance-vendetta, along the lines of "Somebody's going to PAY for this!" Their rage knows almost no limits, and the more damage they can see, the better it makes them feel.

It is the result of systematically sadistic parenting, in an "apprenticeship" manner.

SOCIAL ABUSE (Systematically isolated them from and/or humiliating them with other people)

"You're MINE!" They have no intention of ever letting their child(ren) grow away from them. They will go to almost any extreme to see to it that their child(ren) never have any social contacts or success.

They are the product of an extremely enmeshed or a severely neglecting/rejecting family.

VERBAL ABUSE

"Character assassination." They systematically devastate their child(ren)'s self-respect, self-confidence and self-worth. They intend consciously or not to totally undermine and prevent them from becoming a functional human being.

They were subjected to the same treatment, and they are passing it on.

"ABUSIVE POWER-TRIPPNG" PARENTING PATTERN

"Under my thumb." They WILL be the top dog, no matter what, and they are being especially certain of that with regard to their child(ren). It is a pattern that got started in a similar family culture.

"ACCOUNTABILITY-AVOIDING" PARENTING PATTERN

"It's not my fault!" They systematically duck out from and deflect any and all responsibility for anything that happens around them, and they do the same with their child(ren), who then end up feeling accountable for all evils in the world.

It comes from having grown up in a similar and/or a highly accusatory family.

"ACCUSING" PARENTING PATTERN

"Who's responsible for THIS!?" They are extremely accountability-tracking for purposes of punishment-meeting in an "avenging angel" psychology. They are the product of a similar family.

"ADDICTIVE" PARENTING PATTERN

"Lost in the quest." They are so totally obsessed with the addictive process that all else falls by the wayside, including their child(ren)'s needs. They are incapable of concern and consideration.

It is, of course, the resultant of a severe addiction-induction parenting pattern in their childhood.

"ADOPTING CHILDREN" COMPULSION

"Love-starvation." They are so emotionally deprived that they have become totally dependent upon having children around them at all times to "hold back the oceanic grief."

They are the product of intensely withholding and distant parenting.
****

"Rescue-tripping." They are trying to compensate for their sense of having been "abandoned by God." It arises from having grown up in a severely dysfunctional family, and from feeling that they were "left on a dreadful desert island."
****

"Power-tripping." They simply have to have a group to "lord it over." At the same time, they also have to have the trappings of respectability. It is a pattern that got started when they were systematically dominated and exploited as a child.
****

"Prestige-freak." They are addicted to being the "biggest" and the "best" and the "most." So they have taken up adopting needy children. They come from a severely narcissistic and narcissistically wounding family.

"AGGRESSIVE" PARENTING PATTERN

"Steamroller." They are intensely assertive and explosively reactive in all they do. They figure that "might is right," and they act accordingly. They come from a family in which such tactics were required for their survival.

"AGGRESSIVE-OPPRESSIVE" PARENTING PATTERN

"Snidely Whiplash." They run their family like a slave ship, just like when they were a child.

"ALARMING" PARENTING PATTERN

"You're scaring me!" They lead an at-the-edge lifestyle in which many deeply disturbing events and developments occur. They live life "in the fast lane," and it thoroughly "shakes up the kids."

It is a pattern designed to deflect the deep-seated depression arising from their neglectful childhood.

"ALCOHOLIC" PARENTING PATTERN

"I can do no wrong!" They are constantly engaged in self-destructive and distortedly defensive behavior, including the "Jekyll-Hyde" pattern, with predictably disastrous effects on their child(ren). It is the resultant of severely neglectful and dysfunctional parenting.

"ALICE IN WONDERLAND" PARENTING PATTERN

"Through the looking glass." They live in another world from everyone else, and they act on it. Their child(ren) therefore never know what reality is or if reality is operative at any given point.

It is the resultant of a mind-warping and reality-distorting childhood of the parents.'

"ALWAYS KEEP 'EM GUESSING!" PARENTING PATTERN

"Secret agent." They have an abiding profound distrust of everyone and everything, and they regard their child(ren) as particularly suspect because of their "moral cretin nature" and their "out of control" potentials.

They are, of course, doing unto others what was done to them.

"AMBIVALENT" PARENTING PATTERN

"I don't know if I want to be here." They have deeply unresolved conflicts and mixed emotions and motives which saturate their parenting process. They are the product of an intensely unclear and multi-directionally motivated family culture that never really got it together.
****

"I want you but I don't want you." They have intensely mixed feelings about being a parent and about parenting their particular child(ren). They are not really sure they want these parameters in their life, a pattern that is the resultant of a "keep them around the old homestead" parenting pattern in their childhood.

"AMORAL" PARENTING PATTERN

"Whatever . . ." They do anything and anything that leads to immediate or other perceived payoffs with no regard to the ecological, personal or interpersonal consequences.

They "grew up like Topsy" in a similar environment. ("Topsy" reared herself)

"ANGER-AVOIDING" PARENTING PATTERN

"Now, now, let's not get out of hand here!" They are terrified of what would happen if anger were ever let loose in their family. It comes from having grown up with severe anger, either suppressed or expressed.

"ANGER-SUPPRESSING" PARENTING PATTERN

"Sit on it!" They are intensely fearful of anger, and they therefore systematically suppress any and all forms of expression of it -- with the result that it manifests all over the place in indirect forms. It is a "passing it on" pattern.

ANGRY/HOSTILE PARENTING RELATIONSHIP DISORDER

"You little poop!" They are intensely resentful of their child's needs and impacts, and they project their own rejected self-parts onto their child, they see their own rejecting parents in the child, and/or they fear the child is threatening their authority and control, and they react accordingly.

They are doing unto others what was done unto them.

"ANGRY" PARENTING PATTERN

"Short fuse." Everything irritates and infuriates them, and there is a lot of explosive and resentful behavior in the family. They are the product of a severely dysfunctional and frustrating family.

"ANTI-SOCIAL" PARENTING PATTERN

"Fuck the world!" Their orientation is one of aggressively angry acting out, preferably with damaging effects. They are on one long furious temper tantrum, and they live out of an infantile tyrannosaurus "high chair tyrant" lifestyle.

They were severely neglected and/or they came up in a supremely selfish and at least an amoral if not an antisocial environment.

ANXIOUS/TENSE PARENTING RELATIONSHIP DISORDER

"Excessive harm-avoidance." They live in fear of catastrophic events and disastrous outcomes, and this anxiety permeates their entire interface with their child(ren). They were made fearful of the world by fearful parents, and they are passing it on.

"APPLE TREE" PARENTING PATTERN

"I'll DIE without you!" They are totally dependent on their child(ren) for their life support, due to deep distrust and self-disgust, so that they don't believe that they can derive their sustenance from any other source.

They are, of course, the product of severely depriving and decimating parenting.

"APPRENTICESHIP TRAINING" PARENTING PATTERN

"Next generation." They systematically subject their child(ren) to a subtle and subterranean torture process, and then make alleviation contingent upon compliance and emulation.

It is a pattern that has extended back for generations.

"ASSASSINATION-SEEKING-INDUCING" PARENTING PATTERN

"Overwhelmed and outclassed." They are reacting to their child(ren)'s superior soul development and personal potency with an intense fear and self-suppression-inducing pattern.

They therefore end up producing a pattern in which the individual systematically "points out the emperor's new clothes" in such a manner as to threaten to get themselves terminated. They have the effect of convincing their child(ren) that they are so evil as to require elimination.

They were the product of a massively repressive household.

"ASSAULTIVE" PARENTING PATTERN

"You're in my way!" They take the attitude that anything that bothers them damned well deserves the consequences. They are intensely primitive in their functioning, a pattern they learned at their parents' knees.

"ASSERTION-SUPPRESSING" PARENTING PATTERN

"Don't rock the boat!" They don't want anything to "upset the apple cart," and they therefore insist on the absence of assertiveness in the family. They come from a fearful or an authoritarian family. They are very fear-dominated.

"ASSOCIATE PARENT" or "REVERSED ROLE-REQUIRING" PARENTING PATTERN

"Over-responsibility-demanding." They have high standards of performance and manifestation, and they impose them indiscriminately -- including on their child(ren). They are doing unto others what was done unto them.
****

"Take care of me!" They approach life with the attitude and behavior pattern of one who feels both outclassed and overwhelmed, on the one hand, and that they have the right to demand assistance and privilege, on the other. They are the product of convenience parenting.

"ATTACKING" PARENTING PATTERN

"Lashing out." They react in rage to everything that happens around them, but especially in response to their child(ren). To them, the children are systematically making them miserable, and they therefore deserve punishment and direct reactive feedback.

They come from a severely dysfunctional family, and they have never learned how to understand what is happening in situations and within other people.

"AUTHORITARIAN" PARENTING PATTERN

"Intimate enemy." They are engaged in systematically paranoid parenting that assumes the worst about what everyone is up to, and which derives from an "authoritarian personality." They feel that it is their moral duty to impose their values with a vengeance on their child(ren).

They were, of course, subjected to the same parenting pattern.

"BATTLING BICKERSONS" PARENTING PATTERN

"Fight-aholics." Life is one long argument and angry exchange for them, but at the same time, it is nothing serious. It is just the only way they know how to be intimate, based on modeling from their childhood.

The problem comes in the effects it has on their child(ren), who feel responsible to heal it and to "make it all better," and they can do neither. And they, too, will pass it on to the next generation.

"BELITTLING" PARENTING PATTERN

"Blew it again, eh?" They make fun of, denigrate and discount their child(ren) of an underlying envy and worthlessness feeling derived from similar treatment from their parents.

"BETRAYING" PARENTING PATTERN

"Just when you thought it was safe . . ." They in effect "sell out" their kids like they do everyone else to "get their goodies." They are only concerned with what's in it for them, and the devil takes the hind-most.

It is a pattern that got started in a rather horrifically untrustworthy and massively self-serving family environment.

"BIG STICK" PARENTING PATTERN

"Right and righteous." They consider themselves to be an "avenging angel" who is the guardian of the moral order, and who are therefore justified in whatever enforcement processes they feel are necessary to the cause.

They regard their child(ren) as potentially dangerous and evil, and they act accordingly. They are, of course, doing unto others what was done unto them.

"BLAME-THROWING" PARENTING PATTERN

"NOW look what you've done!" They constantly make their environment accountable and responsible everything that happens to and around them. They come from a family where to be accountable was in effect to be wiped out.

"BOTHERATION" PARENTING PATTERN

"Convenience-concerned." They convey that their child(ren) are a total bother to them. They are unable to connect with and commit to their child(ren), due either to never having had that experience themselves or due to being over-indulged and under-required as a child

"BROKEN BRAIN" PARENTING PATTERN

"You can't do it!" They are convinced that their child(ren) can't take care of the requirements of life, and so they constant do-for, competence-undermine, over-protect, and convey expectations of incompetence.

They are intensely dependent and afraid of losing their child(ren), as a result of being undervalued and denigrated as a child.

"CALCULATING" PARENTING PATTERN

"Quid pro quo." They put everything on a shrewdly self-serving basis with their child(ren). As far as they are concerned, it is strictly a business arrangement in which they get their return or no go.

It comes from having been reared in the same manner, or from having had to come up with this as an approach in their totally uncaring and exploitative family.

"CAPITULATING" PARENTING PATTERN

"Will of spaghetti." They are so uncertain of themselves and where they stand that they are bowled over by anyone who has a strong intention. It is the result of having been thoroughly undermined in their ability to think/see/feel/act for themselves by an authoritarian and/or mind-warpingly self-justifying and wrong-making family.

"CATASTROPHIC" PARENTING PATTERN

"Death and disaster." They lead a calamitous lifestyle that brings about destruction and devastating events routinely. Their parenting pattern is just a reflection of this, and it also reflects their own parenting history as a recipient.

"CATASTROPHIZING" PARENTING PATTERN

"Chicken Little." They fear the worst in every situation, and they are convinced that they see it coming half the time. They particularly take this stance with regard to their child(ren). It is a contagion-based pattern learned in their own childhood.

"CHAOTIC" PARENTING PATTERN

"Random generator." They live a chaos and confusion courting lifestyle that they themselves lived as a child, and they know no better and no other way of being. Nor do they want to, and what's good enough for them is good enough for their grandchildren.

"CHILD-ABUSER"; "CHILD-ABUSING" PARENTING PATTERN

"I just HATE that about you!" (As they turn the finger of blame back on themselves). They are engaged in self-rejection and self-hatred generating "just punishment" behaviors that keep bringing them back to their underlying massive self-revulsion in the form of what they experience as coming from other people, including with their child(ren).

The abusing parent is reacting to projected self-hatred through identification with their child(ren). They are also doing unto others what was done unto them. They have no ability to give love, having never had it themselves.

(See **ABUSIVE PARENTING PATTERN**)

"CHILD-MOLESTING" PARENTING PATTERN

"Mis-guided love." They are highly primitive in their emotional development, and they act out sexually towards those they feel love towards. They mean well, but are severely inappropriate in their love expression.

They are the product of a maturity-undermining and severely dysfunctional family.
****

"Desperately seeking Susan." They are putting the child(ren) in their parent/God/spouse position in an emotional starvation and worth-deprivation reaction. They are trying to heal the devastating impact of severe maternal deprivation, followed by paternal rejection.
****

"Playing doctor." They are in effect an emotional peer of their child(ren), and they are in effect playing with them and/or expressing their affection in a highly inappropriate manner.

They are an emotional child who never got past middle childhood in their development, due to severely invasive mothering. At times, this can be a very loving but hopelessly inadequate fathering situation. They were systematically undermined and infantilized as a child, and they have in effect never gotten out of childhood.
****

"I can't stop myself!" They become "possessed" in either a dissociative and/or an overwhelmingly motivated manner. It is a pattern that got started in their severely sex-ploitative, denial-dominated, suppressive and dysfunctional family.
****

"It's my right!" They are doing unto others what was done unto them, either helplessly as their own pathology takes over or collusively or even proudly, as they manifest their own pathology and devastating history. Sometimes it is reflective of cultural patterns well. It's sometimes called the "Appalachian transplant" situation.
****

"Raging rapist." They have a vengeance/power-tripping mentality in which they are acting out their profound frustration over their effective powerlessness by "lording it over" their child(ren).

It is the resultant of being treated as "special" by a sex-ploitative mother to such a degree that they are in effect derailed from their destiny, and they are out for revenge.
****

"Doing unto others what was done unto them." They are on a sadistic vengeance-vendetta, along the lines of "Somebody's going to PAY for this!" Their rage knows almost no limits, and the more damage they can see, the better it makes them feel.

It is the result of systematically sadistic parenting, in an "apprenticeship training" manner.

(See **CHILD ABUSE**)

"CHILD-NEGLECTOR" PARENTING PATTERN

"Can't cope." They are overwhelmed by life's demands. They are either so competence-anxious that they can't function effectively as a parent and/or they are immersed in a massively survival-threatening situation.

In either case, it is likely to have developed from competence- and confidence-undermining possessive or destructive parenting.
****

"I don't count -- and so you can't either." They have a felt non-deservingness of loving support or even perhaps of the right to live. The neglecting parents are so lost in their own thing that they are unable to provide what is needed for the child.

They are often doing unto others what was done unto them.
****

"Who? You?" They manifest a profound self-immersion and lack of concern for their ecological impact. They are too selfish to even care, much less notice what their child(ren) are going through.

It is the resultant of severely self-immersed "everyone for themselves!" family system.
****

"I can't be bothered -- you little poop!" They are actively hostile towards their child(ren), and they are totally self-immersed to such a degree that they are utterly incapable of doing anything but hurtful things to their child(ren).

They are a ball of fury and hatred towards the world and they profoundly resent any requirements, responsibilities or restrictions on their totally self-feeding lifestyle. If they pay any attention to their child(ren) it is in terms of what the child(ren) can be and do for them only. And they have no conscience or moral feelings about what they do to them.

It is the resultant of intensely hostile cruel treatment as they were growing up that they are in effect beyond reach and completely destructive to anyone in their care.

"CHOSEN ONE" PARENTING PATTERN

"Daddy's little girl, Mommy's little man." They are turning to their child(ren) as their be-all-to-end-all, and they are making sure that they establish an indestructible umbilical connection.

They are too immature to have an adult peer relationship, as a function of being undermined in their coping capabilities as a child.

"CHURCH MOUSE" PARENTING PATTERN

"Passing it on." They are a subtly vicious malicious vengeance-vendetta in action, and they are subjecting their child(ren) to it intensively. They are also "apprenticing" at least one of their children. It is a pattern that goes back for generations.

"COERCIVELY COMPETITIVE" PARENTING PATTERN

"It's a dog eat dog world!" They feel that they have the right to engage in ferocious competitiveness with their child(ren), both because that is all they know, and because they feel that they have to prepare their child(ren) for the world as they know it.

"COERCIVELY CONTROLLING" PARENTING PATTERN

"King of the mountain." They impose their will relentlessly and ruthlessly on their family. They brook no interference, independence or concern for the human race, and they dominate to the point of intimidation.

They have the profound conviction that they are in a control-or-be-controlled world, and they are NOT about to be controlled like they were as a child in their hostile authoritarian family.
****

"Infantile tyrannosaurus." They found out as a two-year-old that they could bully the world, and they continue to do so with their family.

"COLD" PARENTING PATTERN

"Thing-ifying." They treat their child(ren) as "things," and they have little or no capacity for identification, empathy, vulnerability, emotional contact or compassion, all of which were totally absent in their upbringing.

They are "passing it on" and "doing unto others what was done unto them."

"COMMITMENT-AVOIDING" PARENTING PATTERN

"Thou shalt not!" They are unable and/or unwilling to fuse with their child(ren) or to form a lasting deep bond. To them, it would be "parenticide" or "soul-suicide" for not pursuing the "God Housekeeping Seal of Approval" from their withholding parent(s).

"COMPARING" PARENTING PATTERN

"Why can't you measure up to . . . . .?" They are forever comparing themselves to some standard of perfection of performance set by someone else who is world class in an area, out of a profound worth anxiety, and they do the same to their child(ren).

They are forever making invidious comparisons between their child(ren) and between other child(ren) and standards, expectations and other people. They are deeply worth-concerned, and they regard their children as a reflection of how they are doing. They were treated to denigrating and ignoring during their childhood. They are in effect "passing it on."

"COMPETENCE AND CONFIDENCE-UNDERMING" PARENTING PATTERN

"Don't grow away!" They are deeply alarmed at the prospect of the "empty nest" and/or of this child's leaving them. They are intensely dependent on the child, and they therefore systematically sabotage the child's capacity to separate and live successfully in the world.

They are the product of a highly conditional accepting family.
****

"Vicious-malicious." They have a generalized vengeance-vendetta going, and they are targeting their child(ren) in this undermining way as a part of that process. They grew up in a similar family where they were in effect "apprenticed" into the pattern.

"COMPETENCE-UNDERMINING" PARENTING PATTERN

"Keep 'em around the old homestead!" They are afraid of losing their child(ren) and/or they are afraid of the world and its demands, a fear they pass on to their child(ren).

They were given the experience that they don't have what it takes to make it in life as a child.

"COMPETITIVENESS-INDUCING" PARENTING PATTERN

"You *gotta* get ahead!" They have the feeling that if you don't keep continuously "beating out the competition," you will lose out in everything in life. So they systematically encourage, insist on and train their children in the process of "competition to the death."

It comes from being reared in a family in which this was both the philosophy and the reality.

"CONDITIONAL LOVE" PARENTING PATTERN

"You don't deserve love -- you EARN it!" They make it crystal clear to their child(ren) that only if they perform to satisfaction do they get any love from them. They are, of course, passing on what was done unto them.

"CONDITIONAL WORTH" APPROACH, PARENTING PATTERN

"Only if you . . ." was the message they received, and which they continuously give themselves -- and not infrequently others as well. It is of course the direct resultant of having been subjected to severely conditional love parenting.

"CONFIDENCE-UNDERMINING" PARENTING PATTERN

"What makes you think you can do that?" -- "Here, gimme that!" This is the theme song of this family, based on deep distrust of their children. It comes from a perfectionistic and negative assumptive upbringing in their own childhood.

"CONFRONTATION-AVOIDANT AND CONFLICT-AVOIDANT" PARENTING PATTERN

"Anger-avoidance." They are deathly afraid of aggression and alienation, so they avoid confrontation like the plague. They grew up in a severely suppressive and rage-fearing household.
****

"Assertion-avoidance." They are grossly incompetent in assertiveness and aggression, with the result that they "lose out" in situations where these are required. They were systematically competence-undermined as a child.
****

"Passive-aggressive." They are highly fearful of direct confrontation, and they are a past master of indirect undermining and sabotage, as a function of systematic exposure to and training in such processes in their sneakily sadistic family.

"CONFUSION-INDUCING" PARENTING PATTERN

"Incomprehensible." Their functioning doesn't make any kind of discernable sense in many ways, a fact which is majorly impactful on their children. It is a dysfunctional system that results in life seeming to be very confusing.

"CONTINGENT LOVE" PARENTING PATTERN

"Only if . . ." They withhold their "love-line" from their child(ren) as a control strategy and/or to keep them caught up in the "tie that grinds." They are completely submerged in their own needs, and they regard their child(ren) as things to be prevented from hurting them or as desperately desired resources they are not willing to lose.

It comes from having been made extremely insecure about their love lifeline as a child.

"CONTROL-OR-BE-CONTROLLED" PARENTING PATTERN

"Fear of the unknown." They live in nameless terror of "things that go bump in the night," and they absolutely have to have hands-on control of every experience they have, or they go into a paranoid frenzy.

So when it comes to dealing with children, they pass on what was done unto them for the same reasons it was done unto them.

"CONVENIENCE-CONCERNED" PARENTING PATTERN

"Can't see beyond their own fingers and toes." They are developmentally "flat-lined" at a very early age and/or they were under-required and/or over-indulged as a child. They can't take into account more than the immediate hedonic value of things for them. As a result, they are "passing it on" to their child(ren).

"CORKSCREW" PARENTING PATTERN

"Sadistic Snidely Whiplash." They systematically slyly, subtly and subterraneanly "impale" their child(ren) to a corkboard, figuratively speaking, while they convey the message, "If you think THIS is bad, just try and blow the cover or resist it and see what happens!"

It is done in a "singing frog" manner so that if their child(ren) try to "blow the whistle" on the scene, no one sees it, and they pay dearly for it later. Of course, such a pattern usually extends back for generations, and it is taken as "normal" by the family, and the family is taken as "normal" by society, so the child(ren) see no way out of it.

"CORRUPT" PARENTING PATTERN

"Anything goes!" They do what they want when they want it, and they will stop at little to get what they want. They come from a similar family culture, or they were allowed their headstrong and amoral willfulness by a capitulating or convenience-concerned family.

"CRIMINAL" PARENTING PATTERN

"Apprenticeship training." They demonstrate and remonstrate their child(ren) to engage in systematically antisocial and severely destructive self-servingness, backed up with viciousness and violence.

They are of course "passing it on" from numerous preceding generations.

"CRITICAL PARENT" PARENTING PATTERN

"NOW look what you've done!" They have deep-seated resentment and/or perfectionistic expectations that result in their responding to every move their child(ren) make that doesn't fit their desires with strong wrong-making and anger.

It is a pattern that got started from a similar experiential history as a child.

"CRUTCH-AHOLIC" PARENTING PATTERN

"Dysfuctionality personified." They are continuously engaged in "gaminess" and "crutch-grabbing" reality-, responsibility-, accountability- and feeling-avoidance in a totally dysfunctional system. They are the product of a similar family.

"Crutch-aholic" people are very fearful, and they grab the first behavioral/lifestyle "crutch" they can find to lean on as they carry out the resultant pattern of functioning and they try to tolerate the pain of the events and effects of their chosen addictive pattern.

"CYNICAL" PARENTING PATTERN

"Everything sucks!" To them, nothing is worth anything, and everyone is "on the take." They convey this worldview and approach vividly to their child(ren) as being "the way it is" -- with expectable results.

It comes from a similarly oriented family and/or from totally demoralizing life experiences.

"DADDY'S LITTLE GIRL" PARENTING PATTERN

"Come to Papa!" He is subjecting his child to a "spouse substitute" parenting pattern, often involving severe sexualization and not infrequently sexual abuse. He was effectively emotionally castrated by his mother and his abusive or uninvolved father, and he can't form or maintain a successful adult relationship.

"DANCE-AWAY" PARENTING PATTERN

"Tie that grinds." They are totally enamored on and afraid of losing their child, so they put the child on a program of high expectations which constantly elevate, and their child(ren) can never gain their unconditional love or validating approval.

It has the effect of promising "nirvana merging" with the "Home Office" (All That Is) on their child(ren), and it keeps their child(ren) totally caught up in the relationship and unable to commit elsewhere.

They themselves were subjected to the same "carrot-dangle, carrot-yank" parenting pattern, and the beating goes on.

"DEATH IMPLANT-EMBEDDING" PARENTING PATTERN

"If I can't have you, no one can!" They are extremely possessive of and dependent upon their child, and they are subtly installing an injunction for them to summon some form of lethal event if they dare to cross that line towards growing away or leaving them.

It is the resultant of severely confidence- and competence-undermining parenting that effectively destroyed their capacity to believe that they can have love in their life, which generated a huge amount of fulminating fury.

"DEMONIC DYNAMIC" PARENTING PATTERN

"You're being just like my father/mother!" They get into a massively emotional-commotional reactive rage over behaviors and situations with their child(ren) that remind them of the horrors of their own childhood parenting pattern.

"DEMORALIZING" PARENTING PATTERN

"Off their rockers." They are in the grips of severe dysfunctionality to such a degree that it totally unglues the child(ren) with regard to any ability to make sense of or it or to do anything constructive with their life.

They are themselves the product of an equally demoralizingly dysfunctional family.

"DENIAL-DOMINATED" PARENTING PATTERN

"Accountability-avoidance." They don't want to know anything, for fear of having to be responsible for it, and/or for fear of the consequences of being held accountable for it.

They come from a severely dysfunctional and abusively punitive morally oriented family.

"DENIGRATING" PARENTING PATTERN

"There you go again!" They constantly point out to their child(ren) that they are screwing up, and that they are worthless. They are, of course, passing it on from their own childhood experience.

"DEPENDENTLY DEMANDING" PARENTING PATTERN

"You exist to support me." They look to the world around them as a set of potential sources of sustenance. They regard their child(ren) no differently. They were never allowed to develop independent and self-sufficient coping capabilities by their over-indulging and under-requiring family.

"DEPRESSIVE" PARENTING PATTERN

"Overwhelmed and demoralized." They are so wiped out by their depression that they can't carry out the responsibilities of parenting, resulting in the responsibilities being dumped elsewhere -- often onto one or more of their children.

It comes from having been thoroughly demoralized as a child in their dysfunctional or otherwise overwhelming and overweaningly destructive and despair-inducing experiential history.

"DETACHED/DISMISSING" PARENTING PATTERN

"Emotionally unavailable." They minimize or even belittle bonding and attachment, and they are something of a feeling-avoidant "sealed unit" with their child(ren).

They grew up in a distant, emotionally unavailable and uninvolved family.

"DEVALUING" PARENTING PATTERN

"You worthless turd!" They continuously put down their child(ren), in an attempt to bolster their own devastated sense of self-worth, and/or as a function of having been treated the same way as a child.

"DEVIANTLY SELF-JUSTIFYING" PARENTING PATTERN

"I'm right, no matter what!" They systematically twist reality and the facts to support and validate their position and their actions at all costs. They come from a severely manipulative and/or accusative family background.

"DISAPPROVING/JUDGEMENTAL" PARENTING PATTERN

"You can do no right!" They are forever sending the message that what their child is doing is not good enough, not right, or "bad, wrong and evil." They are doing unto others what was done unto them.

"DISORGANIZED/UNRESOLVED" PARENTING PATTERN

"Pin-balling lifestyle." They live their life in a dysfunctional and unpredictable manner that defies planning and comprehension. They are confused and confusing, chaotic in their functioning. They don't understand much of what happens within and around them, and they in essence "try to make a stab at" responding moment to moment.

They are "trapped in the past" of their childhood experience of their "magical mystery-misery tour" environment.

Their child(ren) end up feeling that it's hopeless to ever try to make sense of things or to make anything work effectively. They are passing it on.

"DISSIPATION BLUES" PARENTING PATTERN

"Self-immersed slow suicide." They are self-destructively spiraling out, and they are in effect if not in intention taking their child(ren) with them. They are so self-disgusted and self-negating that they are lost to the systematic self-elimination process, and they can't see anything else than their immediate experience, as they assiduously carry out the apparent "Divine Order" to terminate their "Cosmic disgrace."

They are the product of a severely rejecting, neglecting, self-immersed dysfunctional family.

"DISTRICT ATTORNEYING" PARENTING PATTERN

"All right, where's the rotten core in THIS one?" They operate out of a totally negative assumptive system and experience of life. In their eyes, there is no such thing as a positive or real entity or event. They are deeply suspicious and rageful at their life and the world around them.

It is the resultant of massively destructive dysfunctionality and selfishness in their family. There WAS nothing but poop there. And now they are "passing it on" by doing unto others what was done unto them.

"DOESN'T GIVE -- TILL IT HURTS" PARENTING PATTERN

"Gauging." They withhold attention and involvement until their child(ren) are hurting themselves in some way. Their child(ren) end up feeling that they are somehow "bad," and they act accordingly, in a slow self-destruct lifestyle.

They were subjected to a similar pattern as a child.

"DOMINEERING" PARENTING PATTERN

"Steamrollering." They have to have absolute control of their environment and the events around them, due to a severely paranoid orientation. They are convinced that no one can be trusted, and that they live in an intensely hostile and immoral or amoral world. So they have to "take things into their own hands" and they will "brook no interference." And, of course, their spouse and child(ren) are their "subjects."

They are the product of a paranoid patriarchal authoritarian family in which they were treated as the "intimate enemy" with a "spare the rod and spoil the child" philosophy.

"DON'T MOVE UNLESS I TELL YOU TO!" PARENTING PATTERN

"Strait-jacket pattern." They react to self-expression, environmental exploration, and impact-seeking from their child(ren) with a violent restrictive response intended to keep them totally under control and dominated.

It arises from a profound distrust of the world that was generated by severely repressive/suppressive/oppressive parenting.

"DO THE WORLD A FAVOR AND GO PLAY ON THE FREEWAY!" PARENTING PATTERN

"Demand-avoiding." They have total intolerance of any more requirements and responsibilities than those involved in barely surviving and fending off the next disaster. They are the product of a totally demoralizingly chaotic and devastatingly destructive dysfunctional family.

The result is they have just enough energy and consciousness available to handle the next crisis, period. Anything more is reacted to in a "blindly slashing out" manner. Their response to their child(ren) is one of very intense warning not to force them to the ultimate emergency response -- ostracism and total rejection -- the "go play on the freeway" response.

"DOUBT-RIDDEN" PARENTING PATTERN

"What if . . .?" They are forever lost in potential negative outcomes of any decision or action, and this saturates their parenting style. The result is that there is no structure, and the child(ren) develop all sorts of concerns about potential disasters associated with definitive stand-taking.

It is the resultant of severe wrong-making and/or perfectionistic parenting.

"DRACULA MOM" PARENTING PATTERN

"Psychic vampire." There is a "prana piranha" -- "sucking them dry" impact from her mothering pattern. She is like a "giant walking piece of alum" who in effect "drains the life blood" out of her child(ren), so that they end up looking pale, wan, and on the verge of collapse, with dark areas under the eyes, in what looks like a malnutrition situation, but isn't.

To complicate things further, the mother has a ferociously aggressive defensive approach around any potential interruption of or interference with her "supply line." It is the resultant of having been massively deprived, depraved, degraded and drained as a child. ("Prana" is vital life energy).

"DRAGON'S BREATH" PARENTING PATTERN

"Blast furnace." They are engaged in a chronic irritability and angry interpersonal interface created by a thoroughly frustrating dysfunctional family history. It has resulted in a "This is an up with which I will no longer put!" intolerance reaction to any and all human frailties and failings -- especially in their child(ren), with predictable outcomes.

"DRAMA TRIANGLE" PARENTING PATTERN

"Perpetrator." They are completely caught up in the "Persecutor-Victim-Rescuer" pattern that they learned in their highly dysfunctional family. They have modeled themselves after the power person in their family.

This means that the child(ren) tend to be forced into the powerless positions of the Victim and the Rescuer most of the time, though true to the Triangle form, they sometimes get to play the Persecutor in the process. Once in a while, there occurs an "identification with the aggressor" child who takes on the Persecutor role for life.

In any case, they end up passing it all on.

"DYNAMITE SHED-REACTING" PARENTING PATTERN

"Don't you DARE!" Every time the truth rears its ugly head, they explode apart in a complete disintegration reaction, due to having their desperate denial cover blown. In so doing, they both intimidate-enforce and model the pattern for their child(ren).

They are so utterly terrified of reality that they will do anything to avoid it, and they are completely blown up by being forced to deal with it in any way. They are, of course, a product of a similar family, and they are just "passing it on."

"DYSFUNCTIONAL" PARENTING PATTERN

"Macabre three ring circus." They are dependent, defensive, denial-dominated, disruptive, distorting, disorienting, debilitating, distrust-inducing, deluding, deluging, deteriorating, devastating and death-dealing in their functioning.

They are systematically reality-, responsibility- and accountability-avoidant, as they operate out of the "addictive system," and they are intensely "gamy," with the result that "what you sees is *not* what you gets" in an unconscious and intensely annihilation-anxiety-generating manner.

It is a case of "doing unto others what was done unto them" in their totally dysfunctional family.

"EARLY NEGLECT" PARENTING PATTERN

"Infancy-rejection." They just don't have it in them to be there for an infant, and they aren't. It comes from having had the same experience themselves.

"EGGSHELLING" PARENTING PATTERN

"Appeasing/placating." They have been backed into a "tip-toe-ing through the landmines" pattern by their explosive-coercive and domineering child. Either the child came in with that pattern or they were so intimidated by life that they allowed the child to take over the whole household.

In the latter case, it is the resultant of an extremely explosively assaultive and maniacally controlling family.

"EGO-EXTENSION" PARENTING PATTERN

"Papa's heirloom." They are pinning all their hopes on their child, and the off-spring is given no choice but to follow the program. It is a function of a massive worth-devaluation pattern in childhood.

"EJECTING" PARENTING PATTERN

"Outta here!" They "spit out" the child(ren) who don't "fit in." It comes from the feeling of being threatened by differentness, and by having a "different" child in their family, in a "What will the neighbors think?" pattern.

They come from a highly conformity-emphasizing family background.

"EMOTIONAL COMMOTIONAL" PARENTING PATTERN

"Three ring circus." They are forever going off emotionally, with the associated familial impacts. It is the resultant of growing up in a severely chaotic dysfunctional family.

"EMOTIONALLY VIOLENT" PARENTING PATTERN

"Flailing behavioral machetes." They "let fly with" whatever crosses their guts and mind, and whatever comes out is frequently virulent and vicious. They grew up in a similar system, and they expect and know nothing else.
****

"Subterranean sadism." On the surface, they look wonderful, but underneath, they are a "seething snake pit" of vicious-malicious nastiness, subtle passive-aggressiveness and vengefulness. It results from a severely suppressive, denial-dominated and subtly sadistic family culture.

"EMOTIONALLY WITHHOLDING" PARENTING PATTERN

"The silent treatment." They systematically avoid emotional expression and personal acknowledgement as their means of keeping control of things. It arises from a fundamental underlying deep distrust. It is the resultant of growing up in a thoroughly untrustworthy family.

"EMOTIONAL RECLUSE" PARENTING PATTERN

"Who are you?" They are quite withdrawn and withholding emotionally, especially in close relationships. They are grimly determined not to be emotionally vulnerable to anyone, including their child(ren).

They respond to their child(ren) as the "intimate enemy" who must be guarded against -- with predictable results. It is the product of highly invasive and violating parenting.

"EMPTY NEST" SYNDROME (Freaking out and/or mono-mania reacting to the departure of their child(ren))

"Incomplete life purpose." In our evolutionary history, we didn't live much beyond the child-rearing process. But we live twice as long and growing now, and that leaves many of us (especially women) feeling we have lost our purpose in life after the kids leave.

The resulting reaction understandably involves a lot of grief, despair, anxiety and often anger at the universe. It is, however, not a neurosis. It is a natural reaction to a reality our ancestors did not encounter. It is therefore readily re-workable.

What is needed here is "second stage rocket" counseling for dealing with this life stage process. This is a form of vocational counseling in which you work with a program or with someone to sort out what your skills, resources, passions and situation-survey realities are, in order to commence on your next purposes in life.
****

"Over-identification." They are having an "I'm nothing but . . ." reaction to their child(ren)'s leaving. Their experience is that they are no more than a parent, and they are having something akin to an identity-death reaction.

The response is somewhat like annihilation-anxiety, in which "I" cease to exist. The sense is that they don't have an identity other than that of "The Parent." Their reaction is one of intense alarm and a sense of impending doom (termination). This is a somewhat neurosis-infused version of the "incomplete life purpose" response.

It comes from having been thrust into the "reverse role parent" position as a child.
****

"Socially bereft." For whatever reason, they don't have a circle of friends and the ability to surround themselves with other people. As a result, they become intensely dependent upon their family as their only significant others.

They end up clinging desperately to them out of the fear that they will in effect be all alone if the children leave. They also have an underlying distrust or even fear/awe of other people that keep them alertly apart from people other than those they have been with from the very beginning.

Theirs was an isolated and perhaps insulated childhood where they never learned how to socialize effectively.
****

"Enmeshment." They have built their life around their child(ren), and they are in effect unable to live without them. Furthermore, they have micro-managed and infiltrated their child(ren)'s life so much that their child(ren) can't get away and they themselves can't live without their child(ren). It is an "A-frame" house type of relationship, in which if the one side of the frame leaves, the other collapses.

It comes about as a result of an at best highly conditionally loving parenting, in their childhood, so that they put their child(ren) in the "most rejecting parent" position. In effect, they put all their eggs into that one basket, with all the resulting outcomes. There is likely to have been a similar enmeshment pattern in their family of origin.
****

"Dysfunctional dysphoria." They are the product of a severely ill-working family who left them no option but to become like their parents. This, in turn, led to their developing a uniquely disorganized, emotionally loaded, symbolically dominated and highly aberrant dysfunctional family system in which their children are now an integral part of their whole personal operational system in life.

They react with "cornered rabbit" virulence and even viciousness to their child(ren)'s efforts to leave the family.
****

"Power trip." They are hell-bent-for-leather to detail-dominatingly determine every move their child(ren) makes, and they maintain an authoritarian total control pattern with them.

Their reaction when their child(ren) try to leave is ballistic, and they go into mad mania trying to "show them who's *really* boss." Their feeling is that if they don't have hands on-control of everything around them, it will all go to hell in a hand basket because "Papa/Mama" knows best!

They are the product of an ambulatory paranoid, intimidating and terror-inducing family system.
****

"One and only heir." They were thwarted in their personal ambitions for their life, and so they turn to their child(ren) to live out their unmanifested dreams. They therefore compulsively corner the kid(s) into being what they themselves wanted to be. Their response to the child(ren) leaving to go live their own life is often grotesquely deviant and even demonic.

Not infrequently, this is a multi-generational pattern, in that their family did the same thing to them, or at least their family prevented them from realizing their own dreams.
****

"Incompetent In Living." They never were able to get themselves together as a functional adult and citizen. So when they had kids, they programmed them to fill in for them in all the various aspects of the process of living life.

As a result, they go into something of a severe panic reaction to their child(ren)'s threatening to leave them high and dry. They get desperate as they see various parts of their survival system about to abandon them.

They grew up in a competence- and confidence-undermining family who either had severe self-interest and/or intensely rageful feelings and motivations toward them.
****

"Vengeance-vendetta." Their whole purpose in life as they experience it is to get back for what happened to them as a child. Virtually everything is dealt with as an opportunity-event to "even the score." So when their child(ren) start to leave, they go into a frenzy of envy and rage reaction, and they "give them what they're asking for."

This is a severely virulent personality disorder that requires deep therapy which they are rarely willing to undertake, so beware when encountering this pattern, lest you become the next victim.

It is the resultant of having been treated as the scapegoat for all their parent's hatred for having gone through the same sort of thing when they were a child.
****

"Folie a deux" ("craziness of two"). They have formed a merged psychosis with their child(ren) in which their child(ren) are forced into living out part of their parent's psychosis. And when the child(ren) leave, the individual and their child(ren) manifest full psychotic pattern functioning.

They are the product of an extremely psychotogenic household.

"ENMESHED" PARENTING PATTERN

"A-frame." Relationships of desperate inter-entwinement abound in this family, where everyone is so dependent on everyone else that if anyone pulled out, the rest would collapse in on themselves. They never learned how to function as an independent human being, and so they fashion out of their child(ren) the support systems they need to keep going.

Meanwhile the child(ren) learn that their parents will die if they leave, and they themselves never learn to be whole human beings either, as the pattern gets passed on.

"ENVIOUS" PARENTING PATTERN

"Don 't surpass me!" They are hell-bent-for-leather not to have their child(ren) out-do, out-have, or out-be them, so they systematically undermine their child(ren)'s development, competence, and/or confidence, or they instill in them the fear of God around ever surpassing them.

They come from a viciously competitive and envious patriarchal and perhaps authoritarian household.

"EQUINIMITY-EMPHASIZING" PARENTING PATTERN

"Oil on troubled waters." They are very upset by emotional expression and by intense experiences, and they work very hard at keeping the family "cool as a cucumber."

They come from a severely emotional-commotional or a severely suppressive family. In either case, they dread the "nameless terrors of which they dare not speak" that would happen if things "got out of hand."

"ETERNAL MATERNAL INFERNO" PARENTING PATTERN

"Mama-power!" They approach everything in an "eternal maternal" manner, a "Mama knows best! -- and you had better act accordingly!" approach. They tend to have a "chicken soup" model of everything, and they are guilt-dominated and guilt-inducing, in a wrong-making pattern.

It is the resultant of having had to take over the maternal role in their dysfunctional family when they were a child.

"EXPLOITATIVE" PARENTING PATTERN

"What's in you for me?" They take the approach that everything and everyone is a "mark" for a "score." They are totally self-immersed and self-serving. It is a pattern they learned in a similar family culture.

It can occur on the overt level or on the subtle and subterranean level, depending on the nature of the characteristics of their family of origin and of their current family.

"EXTORTIONISTIC" PARENTING PATTERN

"You'll do it -- or else!" They approach the world in the "alpha male" and the "meanest son-of-a-bitch in the valley" manner. They found out early on in their severely dysfunctional family that this is the way they could get anything they want, and they have never stopped. And they are modeling and coercing it with their child(ren).

"GAMY" PARENTING PATTERN (Slyly destructive and vindictive)
"Nothing is as it seems." They are continuously engaged in various and sundry vengeance and hedonistic reality-avoidance activities, and they subject their child(ren) to the same. It is a "passing it on pattern."

"GOODBAR-RAGE-INDUCING" PARENTING PATTERN (As in "Looking for Mr. Goodbar," the film)
"Destiny-derailing." She systematically undermines her male child(ren)'s capacity for competence and destiny manifestation, while simultaneously appearing to be treating them as "special." It arose from both maternal male-hatred and paternal betrayal.

"GRASS IS GREENER" PARENTING PATTERN
"What's over there!?" They are forever looking for the next "better hit," and they are never able to commit to or to be present to what is as a result. They grew up in a similar family, or in one which was over-indulging and under-requiring, out of convenience-concern or enmeshment. The net effect on their child(ren) is one of generating a never-satisfied and agitated seeking lifestyle.

"GREAT SANTINI" PARENTING PATTERN
"Authoritarian asshole." They are totally egocentric and coercively controlling, with the righteousness of the "judge and jury -- and executioner." They believe that everything they are and stand for is God's Gospel Truth.
They are the "Final Authority," and they are the only one that counts, as far as they are concerned. "My mind's made up. Don't confuse me with facts!" is their motto. This has all the expectable results on who their child(ren) become. It is, of course, the product of a similar family system. ("The Great Santini" was a film about a Marine officer of this type and its effects on his family.)

"GROSSLY INCOMPETENT" PARENTING PATTERN
"In over their head." They are utterly incapable of handling the requirements of parenting, resulting in a calamitously damaging childhood experience for their child(ren). They were thoroughly devastated in their coping capabilities in their neglectful and severely dysfunctional household.

"GUARDIAN OF MORALITY" PARENTING PATTERN
"Hanging judge and jury." They impose their highly intolerant, reductionistic and hostile value and belief system on their vulnerable and impressionable child(ren.) It is a moral crusade for them, reflecting their ambulatory paranoid personality structure.
They are simply passing on what happened to them.

"HARSHLY ATTACKING" PARENTING PATTERN

"What have you done now, you little terd!?" They believe that nobody is up to any damned good, and they take that attitude in dealing with their child(ren). They are the product of a similar family culture.

"HEART-STOPPING MOM" PARENTING PATTERN

"Somebody's going to PAY for what happened to me!" They are striking out in indiscriminate revenge for what was done to them in their childhood, and the result is a parenting pattern that "scares their child(ren) to death."

She actually glees on the impact she has in her blind rage.

"HELICOPTERING" PARENTING PATTERN

"Hovercraft." They hands-on control every aspect of their child(ren)'s life with no ability to let things happen on their own. They are trying to cover everything and to get their child(ren) to "grow up fast." It is an "ego-mirror" self-reflection issue and/or excessive harm-avoidant over-protectiveness. It has the effect of undermining their child(ren)'s ability to live life effectively.

They are the product of highly conditional love parenting with perfectionistic standards. "Do RIGHT or we won't love you!" was the theme of the parenting pattern.

"HIP" PARENTING PATTERN ("Hung up In Principles")

"Papa/Mama knows best!" They do everything out of a set of high-sounding principles and maxims -- including parenting. The problem is they only pay attention to their principles, and not realities and needs. It is a pattern that was passed on from a similar family.

"HOSTILE" PARENTING PATTERN

"You deserve it!" Their general attitude is one of derisive rage and "avenging angel" self-justification for all sorts of virulent and violent viciousness. They are the product of a similar family system.

"HUMORLESS" PARENTING PATTERN

"Tain't funny, McGee!" They have a super-somber, mirthless, dour/sour and negative assumptive/focused approach to life and especially to child-rearing. Their basic stance is that they are to never let the kids "get out of hand" or to fail to see the grim importance of everything.

They are the product of an "American Gothic" family system, (That is the title of that famous work of art with the gruesomely grim farmer, his wife and his pitchfork).

"IF ONLY . . ." PARENTING PATTERN

"Re-hashing." They are forever regretting and ruminating over what might/should/could have been. They deluge their child(ren) with these concerns, in effect passing on their own childhood experience.

"IGNORING" PARENTING PATTERN

"Maybe they'll go away." They are overwhelmed by the requirements of parenting and/or of their particular child(ren), and they are hoping that their progeny will somehow just disappear. They come from a denial-dominated dysfunctional family.

"INCEST PERPETRATOR"

"Misguided love." They are highly primitive in their emotional development, and they act out sexually towards those they feel love towards. They mean well, but they are severely inappropriate in their love expression with their child(ren).

They are the product of a maturity-undermining and severely dysfunctional family.
****

"Playing doctor." They are in effect an emotional peer of their child(ren), and they are in effect playing with them and/or expressing their affection in a highly inappropriate manner.

They are an emotional child who never got past middle childhood in their emotional development, due to severely invasive mothering. At times, this can be a very loving but hopelessly inadequate parenting situation.

They were systematically undermined and infantilized as a child, and they have in effect never gotten out of childhood.
****

"Desperately seeking Susan." They are putting the child(ren) in their parent/God/spouse position in an emotional starvation and worth-deprivation reaction. They are trying to heal the devastating impact of severe maternal deprivation, followed by paternal rejection.
****

"I can't stop myself!" They become "possessed" in either a dissociative and/or an overwhelmingly motivated manner. It is a pattern that got started in their severely sex-ploitive, denial-dominated, suppressive and dysfunctional family.
****

"It's my right!" They are doing unto others what was done unto them, either helplessly, as their own pathology takes over, or collusively, or even proudly, as they manifest their own pathology and devastating history in a "passing it on" situation.

Sometimes it is reflective of a cultural pattern as well, as in the "Appalachian transplant" pattern.
****

"Raging rapist." They have a vengeance/power-tripping mentality in which they are acting out their profound frustration over their effective powerlessness by "lording it over" their child(ren).

It is the resultant of being treated as "special" by a sex-ploitive mother to such a degree that they are in effect derailed from their destiny, and they are out for revenge.
****

"Doing unto others." They are on a sadistic vengeance-vendetta, along the lines of "Somebody's going to PAY for this!" Their rage knows almost no limits, and the more damage they can see, the better it makes them feel.

It is the result of systematically sadistic parenting, in an "apprenticeship training" manner.

"INCOMPETENCING" PARENTING PATTERN

"Failure-programming." They are systematically preventing the development of and undermining the ability for self-sufficiency and success. It comes from envy, dependency and/or vengeance arising from being subjected to the same treatment when they were a child.

"INCOMPETENT" PARENTING PATTERN

"Flat-out unable." Things have broken down in the parenting process, and they are engaging in non-optimal parenting practices. They are in part reflecting the lack of effective parenting they received, and in part, they are "passing it on" from their own childhood experience.

"INDIFFERENT" PARENTING PATTERN

"Whatever . . ." Their attitude is that nothing really matters, including their child(ren). They are totally demoralized and amoral in their approach, as a function of having grown up in a similar family.

"INFANTILZING" PARENTING PATTERN

"Helplessness-inducing." They are so afraid of people and of losing their "mothering" role that they are systematically interference-running, do-for-ing and non-requiring of their child(ren) to such an extent that the child(ren) are effectively helpless without her.

They were denied love and support as a child to an extreme degree. This child or these children are the first person(s) they have ever had love from. There may well also be a cruel vengeance component to the pattern, of a projective identification nature, where they are "punishing themselves."

"INJUSTICE-NURTURING" PARENTING PATTERN

"Pervasive bitterness." They are intensely disillusioned, disgusted and distrusting of everything, and they are passing it on to their child(ren). It arises from similar parenting, and the beat goes on.

"INSENSITIVE" PARENTING PATTERN

"Egocentric blindness." As parents, they operate like a "runaway Mack truck," a "walking cadaver," a "hung up in principles" irrelevant, an "egghead," a "super-selfish," etc. They are so self-immersed that they can't see the impact they have on their ecology.

They were treated the same way by their parents.

"INTERFERENCE-RUNNING" PARENTING PATTERN

"Blocker." They prevent their child(ren) from experiencing the natural consequences of their actions, with the result that they systematically undermine their child(ren)'s capacity to function effectively. It comes from either possessive enmeshment and/or passive-aggressive effectence-devastation motivations.

It arises from a severely dysfunctional parenting pattern that effectively prevented them from developing mature functioning capabilities, and they are now in effect passing it on.

"INTIMATE ENEMY" PARENTING PATTERN ("Spare the rod and spoil the child," "Assume the worst," "Believe only your own convictions," etc.)

"Control or be controlled!" -- "Dog eat dog world!" -- "ambulatory paranoid" orientation. They regard children as unsocialized monsters who have to be "brought under control."

They therefore exercise highly harsh procedures, and they harbor intensely negative assumptions about the motivations and potential developmental implications of everything their child(ren) are and do.

They are doing unto others what was done unto them.

"INTIMIDATING" PARENTING PATTERN

"Might is right." They run their family on the basis of the "meanest son of a bitch in the valley gets the goodies." They are simply "passing it on."

"INTRA-UTERINE REJECTION" PARENTING PATTERN

"Can't handle it." They are overwhelmed and horrified by being pregnant and they are acting on it emotionally and physiologically. They are in circumstances that generate this reaction, whether that is having had the same experience in the womb and beyond, and/or by being in totally untenable circumstances at this time.

"INTRUSIVE" PARENTING PATTERN

"EVERYTHING is my business!" They stick their nose into everything for their own purposes, and with their own interpretations. They were treated the same way, and they figure it is everyone else's turn, now that they are the power figure.

"INVASIVE" PARENTING PATTERN

"Battering ram." They coercively force their way into every situation and into everyone's psyche with a moralistic "avenging angel's" intensity. They are on a "moral crusade" against "all the scum of the world."

They are the product of a virulently vicious and emotionally violent family, who engaged in the same tactics.

"JEKYLL-HYDE" PARENTING PATTERN

"Quick-change artist." They are unpredictably explosive and violent-virulent, with the result that their child(ren) never knew what to expect and when. It is the product of severely suppressive and dysfunctional parenting.

"JOCASTA COMPLEX" –INDUCING PARENTING PATTERN (Castrating enmeshment by the mother in particular) ["Jocasta" was Oedipus' mother]

"Don't you DARE grow away!" They are being exploitative, abusive and rejecting by threatening to abandonment-annihilate or in other ways destroy their child(ren) if they own their value and potency, and/or by giving them the message that to do so would destroy the parents.

They were effectively neglected and exploited in a similar family.

"JUDGEMENTAL" PARENTING PATTERN

"J'accuse!" They assume the worst about everything associated with their child(ren), and they pass judgment on everything they are and do. They are the product of a similar family system.

"KEEP THEM AROUND THE OLD HOMESTEAD" ("KAOH") PARENTING PATTERN

"A-frame dependency." They are continuously incompetence-, immaturity- and self-immersion-generating, and they are "do-for-ing," interference-running, over-indulging and under-requiring.

They are also likely to systematically program in self-defeating and alienation-inducing patterns, so as to lead to rejection of the individual in the larger world. They are seeking to guarantee that their child(ren) will never want or be able to leave them.

It is based on abandonment-anxiety, -- they feel unable to cope without their "parent stand-ins," so they do what they can to keep them home "where they belong," often on a subconscious level.

It is the resultant of systematic competence- and confidence-undermining parenting in their own childhood.

"LACK OF COMPASSION" PARENTING PATTERN

"Super-selfish." They experience and evaluate everything in terms of how it affects them, and that includes their dealings with their child(ren). They never got past the basic survival level in their emotional development, due to the dysfunctionality of their family.

"LACK OF UNDERSTANDING" PARENTING PATTERN

"Simplistic." They are lost in their own needs and in concretistic thinking about everything. They are therefore incapable of comprehending their child(ren)'s experiences, needs or situations.

They were developmentally "flat-lined" at a very early level of survival basics functioning, due to the dysfunctionality and/or impoverishment of their family.

"LADY MADONA" PARENTING PATTERN

"Self-prostituting." They are engaged in a lifestyle which ignores their impact on their significant others, their child(ren) in particular. They were simultaneously withheld from and attacked for being a "slut" by sex-ploitative and abusive parents.

So they are embarked on a "prove them right" self-destructive spiral that is unconcerned with anything else or with their ecological effects.

"LITTLE LORD FAUNTLERY" PARENTING PATTERN

"My perfect angel!" She was profoundly disappointed and damaged by her father's authoritarian, exploitative or seductive-destructive pattern. She ended up desperately needing validation, completion and reciprocation from an important male.

Unfortunately, she in essence married her father, and she found herself shaping up her childishly idealized image of the man she wanted in her life in her son. And of course he ended up all-too-willingly falling into the pattern.

"LOVE-AHOLIC" PARENTING PATTERN

"Will you love me tomorrow?" They are intensely abandonment-anxious, and they therefore continuously monitor what their social environment is doing in response to them for signs of immanent disaster. This includes their children, of course, and they subject them to constant clinging and enmeshment. They were subjected to similar treatment.

"LYING LOW" PARENTING PATTERN

"Trying to disappear." They desperately don't want to be noticed, due to having come up in a severely authoritarian and violent family. And they are passing it on by doing the same thing to their child(ren).

"MACHO MOM"

"Mad maternal." They engage in never-ending interference-running, hyper-nurturing, over-protective, under-requiring, over-indulgent, and do-for artist mothering. They display unlimited pity and measureless sympathy, which has the effect of being infantilizing and disempowering to those upon whom she focuses her super-support.

It comes from having been thrust into this role by their intensely symbiotically dependent family.

"MANIPULATIVE" PARENTING PATTERN

"Whatever it takes . . ." Their attitude is that all's fair in love and war, which to them are almost synonymous. They end up modeling and teaching their child(ren) to do the same.

It comes from having grown up in such a family, and they are clearly passing it on.

"MATERNAL SABOTAGE" PARENTING PATTERN

"Self-commitment-sabotaging." They are engaged in systematic undermining and/or derailing of self-manifestation in their child(ren). It arises out of desperate abandonment-anxiety generated by severely ambivalent or rejecting parenting.
****

"Self-sabotaging." They are consistently self-undermining, in response to maternal programming to never grow away. It is due to an intense "keep them around the old homestead" parenting pattern and they are passing it on.

MIXED PARENTING RELATIONSHIP DISORDER

"Dysfunctional Dolly/Daddy." They manifest all the disorders of parenting in an unpredictable mélange. They are passing on the kind of parenting they received.

"MOMMYING WOMAN" (Doing and determining everything in a disempowering manner -- especially with her son[s])

"Engulfing." She has as a deep-seated motivation "keeping them around the old homestead." To do so, she enmeshes him in everything she does, and she involves herself in everything they do.

She has a profound abandonment-anxiety and fear of standing alone on her own arising from a severely enmeshing and competence/confidence-undermining family.
****

"Incompetencing." She runs interference and intervenes constantly in everything her child(ren) do so that they are incapable of independent functioning. She is both desperately dependent on them and seethingly resentful of them for every aspect of her parent(s) that they manifest.

She was severely damaged by an indifferent, abandoning, sexualizing and/or cold/cruel family.
****

"Tripod-rage." She is intensely misanthropic, and in her mind, no man can ever do anything right. She continuously criticizes, devalues and accuses her son about everything. She comes from a family in which her mother hated everything masculine due to severe abuse and/or exploitation by her father and/or by the mad male within her mother.
****

"Castrating." She systematically undermines her son's competence, confidence and self-respect. She is out to in effect "do him in" so that he can never function in an effective or masculine manner. She is on a vengeance-vendetta for what her father did to her. She may also be involved in "masculine protest," in which she wants to prove to her father that "she is a better man than he is."
****

"Destructive." She is a virulently hostile woman who slashes, gashes and smashes everyone in her path. She has it particularly in for her son(s) because of the heavy-handed handling she got from her father. Meanwhile, her super-vicious sneaky sadist mother was the mastermind of all the mayhem.

"MOMMY'S LITTLE MAN" PARENTING PATTERN

"Now YOU'RE the man in my life!" She is doing a spouse-substitute parenting pattern with their child, often including sexualization and perhaps even sexual abuse on a continuously invasively erotic basis.

She was devastated by her father and her mother was intensely possessive, so she can't form true adult relationships.

"MORAL MONSTER" PARENTING PATTERN

"Prison guard." They regard children as unsocialized sociopaths who require continuous training in morality and discipline, lest they get away without becoming truly human. So they are forever pouncing and pounding on them "for their own good." They are, of course, passing it on and doing unto others.

"MOTHERS WHO LOVE TOO MUCH" PARENTING PATTERN

"And kids who can't defend themselves." The child(ren)'s mother expresses her love the way she was taught that love is to be expressed -- and it is devastating in its impact.

She is, of course, passing on what was done unto her.

MUNCHAUSEN SYNDROME (Inducting physical illnesses in oneself for attention)

"I need help!" They work at being able to play the "sick" role. They continuously feign and develop physical symptoms for the sole purpose of being medically treated.

They typically don't work or take care of themselves. They go to extremes and they become addicted to hospitalization, surgery, medication, etc. It is an extremely exaggerated extension of the "staying home from school to get the attention they never got" syndrome.

They were in effect totally ignored unless they got sick in the context of a psychosis-inducing intensely pathological, narcissistic and massively neglectful and cruel family, who modeled self-immersed manipulation to the point where it became their whole nature.

"FATALISTIC" PARENTING PATTERN

"What's the use?" They have the distinct experience that no matter what they do, it's all going down the tubes anyway. They are the product of a demoralizingly dysfunctional family, and they are doing a good job of passing it on.

"FAVORITISM" PARENTING PATTERN

"Daddy's little girl, Mommy's little man." They are turning to their child(ren) as their be-all-to-end-all, and they are making sure that they establish an indestructible umbilical connection.

In the process, they are oblivious to or they ignore the impact it is having on the chosen child's siblings. They are too immature to have an adult peer relationship or to be ecologically concerned, as a function of being undermined in their coping capabilities as a child.

"FEARFUL" PARENTING PATTERN

"Chicken Little." They are operating out of continuous catastrophic expectations in a highly contagious manner that gets passed on to their child(ren), just like it was to them.

"FEELING-SUPPRESSING EMOTIONAL WITHOLDING" PARENTING PATTERN

"Playing it close to the chest." They are intensely fearful of letting their emotions loose, and they therefore hold everything back, in a self-inhibiting non-self-disclosive manner.

It is the product of a repressive dysfunctional family in which any form of emotional expression was the occasion for massive punishment or other severely negative outcomes.

"FOG-BOUND" PARENTING PATTERN

"Iron-fisted ghostly presence." They are forever lost in space in a "fog" of hydrochloric acid vapor, with the result that they have an absolute mania for hands-on control run by their distorted interpretation system.

They are the product of virulently vicious, thoroughly confusion-inducing, and cognition-devastating parenting.

"FOLIE A DEUX-INDUCING" ("Craziness of two") PARENTING PATTERN

"Addicted to their child." They are totally symbiotically attached to their off-spring, and they systematically denigrate and totally undermine all possibility of attachment to outside resources for the child.

It arises from having been thoroughly demoralized about their inability to cope, due to severely competence- and confidence-undermining parenting.

"NEGATIVITY-DEFLECTING" PARENTING PATTERN

"Minimize your losses" is the motto of this family. They have an underlying conviction that there is nothing one can do that will be constructively improving of their situation, they can only keep the damage down as much as possible.

They are the product of an overwhelmingly dysfunctional family.

NEGLECT OF CHILD (Perpetrating adult)

"Lost in their own concerns." They are having a "WHAT kid!?" reaction to being a parent. They are so self-immersed and/or overwhelmed that they can't remember the needs of their child(ren).

They are unable to rise to the challenge, uncaring, completely caught up in their own world, or in other ways totally oblivious or unequipped to provide concern and nurturance to their child(ren).

In so doing, they are passing on what happened to them, and they are doing unto others what was not done unto them. It is the resultant of severely depriving and destructive dysfunctional parenting in their childhood.

"BENIGN NEGLECT" PARENTING PATTERN

"That's nice, dear." They are something of a "sealed unit" who lives out their own lifestyle, with relatively little notice of or concern for their child(ren)'s needs.

They have the experience that they have to take care of themselves, because no one else will, because that is what happened to them as a child.

"NEVER GOOD ENOUGH" PARENTING PATTERN

"Impossible standards." They operate out of perfectionist performance expectations, as reflections on the parents' worth and acceptability. It is a passing on of their parents' "sentence."

"NIHILISTIC" PARENTING PATTERN

"What's the use?" They operate out of a hopeless and disparaging attitude, and they systematically subject their children to this orientation. They come from a severely dysfunctional family in which nothing ever worked.

"NIRVANA-PROMISING" PARENTING PATTERN

"Hopelessly hooked." They are totally dependent upon their child(ren), and they are afraid of losing them. But they are also afraid of losing their similarly nirvana-promising parent (who to them is God, at the gut level). [Nirvana is fusion with God]

For both reasons, they can never let their child(ren) "have" them, so they always jerk the "golden orb" at the last minute with "not good enough" messaging.

They are the product of a similar situation.

"NON-ACCEPTING" PARENTING PATTERN

"You don't belong here!" Their attitude towards their child(ren) is one of not being willing to deal with the reality of their existence and their needs. The children feel like an imposition from the Universe or from someone else that they never agreed to. They feel at the mercy of the world, and they deeply resent it.

It arises from a childhood in which their needs came last.

****

"Who are *you?*" Children don't figure into their lifestyle. They are totally self-immersed, and the requirements of children are extremely irrelevant and alien to them. They were largely convenience-concerned parented, and they are passing it on.

"NO ROOM FOR YOU!" PARENTING PATTERN

"Ignoring their existence." They treat their child(ren) as if they weren't there, because they desperately wish they weren't. They feel outclassed and overwhelmed, or they are too self-immersed to be bothered with the needs of children.

They were either undermined in their ability to cope, or they were over-indulged to the point where they could not cope or contribute.

"NOW LOOK WHAT YOU'VE DONE!" PARENTING PATTERN

"Inconvenience-hating." They are engaged in a convenience-concerned and/or a harm-avoidant parenting pattern arising from self-immersion. It can happen out of a variety of causes, but functionally, they explode in rage and accusation when things go wrong.

They are the product of severely self-immersed parenting.

"NUMBINGLY DESTRUCTIVE" PARENTING PATTERN

"Battering to oblivion." They are living such a devastatingly destructive lifestyle that their child(ren) have no choice but to numb out to survive it all. They are the product of similar circumstances.

"ONE AND ONLY HEIR" PARENTING PATTERN

"You gotta do it MY way!" They impose their intended destiny and thwarted ambitions and expectations on their child(ren). They build their whole life around their child(ren) doing what they can't and desperately want to accomplish and experience. They are incapable of empathically understanding their child(ren)'s experience, needs or desires.

They are the product of a severely patriarchal and authoritarian family.

"OPPRESSIVELY UPBEAT" PARENTING PATTERN

"Speak no evil." They are intensely fearfully denial-dominated and "shadow-shoving" in their functioning and in their family culture. It is a resultant of a severe fear of what would emerge if they got in touch with their darker side.

They grew up in a ferociously suppressive family.

"OUT OF SYNC" PARENTING PATTERN

"Bad dancer." They are just not in tune with their child(ren)'s "dance of life," and everything they do is not fitted to what is happening with their child(ren). It is, of course, a "passing it on" pattern.

"OVER-ACCOMODATING" PARENTING PATTERN

"Over-responsible." They are intensely concerned for the welfare of everyone and every situation they encounter. They were the "family host" in their self-defeatingly dysfunctional and exploitative family.
****

"Eager to please." They are highly rejection-anxious, and they desperately want to be liked. So they rush to fulfill every indication of desire or need on the part of other people. They grew up in a highly conditionally accepting and rejecting family.
****

"Serve-aholic." They are excessively responsive and responsible, feeling that it is their total requirement to meet the needs and desires of everyone, every situation and every system they encounter.

They are emotionally convinced that they have to "make up for" their "evilness" by compulsive service. They were held accountable for everything that went wrong in their dysfunctional family.
****

"Me last!" They have a compulsively self-denying and need/want/wish-filling propensity which accompanies a pronounced tendency to consider *their* needs, wants and desires to be undeserved, unimportant and/or bad, wrong and evil.

They come from a highly exploitative, denigrating, dysfunctional and perhaps abusive family.
****

"Edith Bunker." They are highly dependent upon the creative initiative of others to be able to manifest and create. They are either intensely yin in their essence and/or they were yang-suppressed or de-masculinized by their family.
****

"Anything you say." They are totally afraid of conflict, confrontation and attack, and they are therefore massively compliant to the requirements of systems, situations and people.

They are the product of a severely abusive and coercive dysfunctional family.
****

"Self-suppressing." They are in effect afraid to release themselves in any way, and they go out of their way not to impose, alienate or upset others via continuously adjusting to other people's needs/wants/desires.

They come from an oppressive and authoritarian household.
****

"Crushed coke can." They are extremely self-oppressing to the point of being in effect unable to self-express, to initiate or to strike out on their own direction. They were overwhelmingly "steamrollered" by their fulminatingly furious, paranoid and/or authoritarian family.
****

"Seething volcano." They sit on themselves to such a degree that they are utterly infuriated. They are far too afraid of themselves and of the world to every "let go with themselves."

Their family was severely suppressive and sadistic.
****

"Lying in wait." They make it a point to not be noticeable as they scheme and scam to get their "pound of flesh" for each and every "violation" they experience. They are the product of a severely vengeful and sneakily sadistic family.

"OVER-ACHIEVEMENT-PUSHING" PARENTING

"Brass ring-chasing." They are forever pressuring their child(ren) to outperform others and themselves. Their child(ren) are their ego-extensions, and they are desperate to come out as "Number One."

They were severely narcissistically wounded by their achievement-pushing, perfectionistic and/or "never good enough" parenting.

"OVER-INDULGING" PARENTING PATTERN

"Don't bother me!" It is a "Here, take this" parenting pattern born out of intensely self-immersed concerns. They were treated the same way, and they are just passing it on.
****

"Don't leave me!" They in effect seek to "buy" the never-ending involvement and support of their child(ren) by showering them with compliance and gifts. They are terrified of facing life on their own, and they can't be involved in an adult relationship, due to severe competence-undermining as a child.

"OVER-INTELLECTUAL" PARENTING PATTERN

"Walking cerebrum." They are massively feeling-avoidant and reality-deflecting in their functioning, wanting instead to impose their mental model of the world onto everything. They are the product of a severely dysfunctional and denial-dominated family in which they found that the "walking cerebrum" defense was the best way to survive.

"OVER-INVOLVED" PARENTING DISORDER

"Ego-extension." They are strongly inclined to see their child(ren) as their resources to meet their own needs, not those of the child(ren), and they utilize them accordingly. They are intrusive, domineering, eroticizing, confidante-demanding, and under-interactive with their child(ren).

They are developmentally "flat-lined" very early in life, and they are forcing their child(ren) to sustain them at that level.

"OVER-PROTECTIVE" PARENTING PATTERN

"Maturation-prevention." They run interference, under-require, over-indulge, and in general prevent their child(ren) from learning how to cope with life. It arises either out of possessiveness of the child, in which case they are trying to "clip their wings" so they can't fly away, or out of fear of harming them, due to assumed or real disability on their child(ren)'s part.

"OVER-REACTIVE" PARENTING PATTERN

"Chicken Little." They react to everything as if it was the end of the world with their child(ren). They are terrified of the process of life and of the Universe, and they feel totally unequipped to cope.

It has the effect of turning off their child(ren) to the point where they don't listen to them -- at times leading to serious endangerment or detriment to them. They are the product of an emotional-commotional, disorganized and alarmingly dysfunctional family that made them feel overwhelmed and endangered at all times.

"OVER-RESPONSIBLE" PARENTING PATTERN

"It's all up to me!" They feel personally responsible for everything and they have to "make up for" all that has gone wrong in the world, as if it was all their doing. They also feel they have to prevent all harm happening to their children.

It arose out of being expected to "make everything all better" when they were a child, and when they couldn't, they were accused of causing all the evils of the world.

The pattern got started in a combination of the individual's being superior in some way in the context of a great deal of need and rage on the part of their parents.

"OVERWHELMED" PARENTING PATTERN

"I just can't keep up." They find that they simply don't have the wherewithal to handle the requirements of parenting, and they are in effect "throwing in the towel" on the whole operation.

They were so undermined in their coping capabilities as a child and/or they have encountered such intensely demanding circumstances that they have had to "cut their losses."

"PALSY-WALSY" PARENTING PATTERN

"Dear Prudence." They in effect want a playmate, not the responsibilities involved with their own child(ren). They have never grown up, and they want to remain "forever young," and they are using their child(ren) as the means to keep the delusion going.

They were of course prevented from maturing as a child.

"PARENTAL ALIENATION SYNDROME" (PAS) [Systematic turning their child(ren) against the other parent]

"My way or the highway!" They are highly prone to operating out of their own reality, and to take on things for their own gain. They mount assaults on the world to try to "prove" their view and to get what they want.

Unfortunately, what they want is so bound up in their personal pathology that it becomes a madman's ecological impact. To make matters worse, their "own reality" picture of everything gives them utter conviction and convincingness, resulting in their often persuading or misleading everyone to their view of things, which they then exploit intensely for their own objectives.

It is the resultant of a reality-distorting and power-abusing parenting that disrupts their ability to perceive reality or to be concerned about their ecological impact. They end up coercing the world to buy into their version of things, and each successful event massively re-validates their quasi-delusional and effectively unprincipled pattern.

PARENT-CHILD RELATIONAL PROBLEM

"Incompetent parenting." Things have broken down in the parenting process, and they are engaging in non-optimal parenting practices. They are in part reflecting the lack of effective parenting they received, and in part, they are "passing it on" from their own childhood experience.

"PARENTICIDE-PARANOIA-INDUCING" PARENTING PATTERN

"Betrayal-paranoia." The parent is so deathly afraid that their child will abandon them that they induce in their child(ren) a deep fear of what would happen to the parent if their child(ren) manifest their potency, identity or destiny.

They are the product of severely competence- and confidence-undermining parenting.

"PARIAH PATTERN-INDUCING" PARENTING PATTERN

"Overwhelmed and outclassed." They respond to the superior soul development of their child(ren) by putting them on a "self-checkmating" and alienation-inducing pattern, as a means of controlling them.

They are the product of a severely suppressive household.

"PASSIVE-AGGRESSIVE" PARENTING PATTERN

"Nothing is as it seems." Theirs is a family system in which much subterranean sabotage continuously occurs. They are on a generalized vengeance-vendetta, but it has to be kept out of sight and awareness, so it comes out in mediated, indirect and time-lapsed episodes over and over again. They learned it in their family of origin, who were doing the same thing.

"PASSIVELY IRRESPONSIBLE" PARENTING PATTERN

"Let George do it." They are forever doing a "passing the buck" number. They function like a responsibility-ducking bureaucrat. It comes from their having grown up in a self-immersed family system, or with an under-requiring "keep them around the old homestead" parenting pattern.

"PATRIARCHAL" PARENTING PATTERN

"Father knows best!" They run their family like a military academy, and they expect everyone to jump to their command. They are the product of a similar family.

"PEDESTALIZING" PARENTING PATTERN

"Extreme role-reversing." They are looking for the "perfect parent," usually the ideal mother, who will be someone they rely on totally for their protection, instruction and direction.

They feel "cast adrift with insufficient equipment" and "cheated out of their birth-right" to have an idealization resource upon which to draw in their functioning, and to which to turn for solace. It is a desperate attempt to make up for significant maternal deprivation and/or neglect.

Unfortunately, it puts their child(ren) in an impossible demanding situation that often leads to self-destructive patterns.

"PERFECTIONISTIC" PARENTING PATTERN

"Perform or else!" They expect their children to rise to their standards before they will give any love. They are passing on what happened to them.

"PERFECTIONISTICALLY PUNISHING" PARENTING PATTERN

"Not one iota!" They systematically reject and punish their children for any deviation from absolute perfection of performance. It arises from profound worthlessness feelings generated by similar parenting.

"PERFORMANCE-DEMANDING" PARENTING PATTERN

"Perform or else . . . we won't love you!" They regard public presentation and performance perfection as the ultimate indicators of their worth, and they demand of their child(ren), who are seen as stand-ins for them in the world's eyes.

They also regard performance as the bottom line of survival. For both reasons, they demand perfection of performance from their child(ren). They were, of course the recipients of the same process.

"PETER PAN(ELLA)" PARENTING PATTERN

"I won't grow up!" They utterly refuse to take on adult responsibilities, and they operate out of the pleasure principle at all times. This has the effect of forcing their child(ren) to reverse roles and parent them as well as taking care of things.

They were over-indulged and under-required as a child in their enmeshed and doting family.

PHYSICAL ABUSE OF CHILD (Perpetrator)

"Passing it on." The parent(s)' general orientation is either that it is the only thing that works, or it is all that they can do on the one hand, or that it worked for them and for generations back and for everyone else, on the other. In both cases, the "chain of pathology" continues.
****

"Projective identification." They are caught up in self-rejection and self-hatred, thereby generating "just punishment" behaviors (beyond the initial period of the abuse). The perpetrator is reacting to projected self-hatred onto the child. They are also doing unto others what was done unto them. They have no ability to give love, having never had it themselves.

(See "ABUSIVE" PARENTING PATTERN)

PHYSICALLY ABUSIVE PARENTING RELATIONSHIP DISORDER

"You're doing it to me!" They are projecting onto their child(ren) what their parents did to them, and they are acting out the rage and resentment they had as a child towards their child(ren).

There is also an element of projective identification, where they attack those parts of themselves that they hate by projecting them onto their child(ren).

(See **"ABUSIVE" PARENTING PATTERN**)

"POISON APPLE" PARENTING PATTERN

"Grossly untrustworthy." They consistently display destructive behavior towards their child(ren) -- their "love" contains "razor blades" or "poison." It is a form of "doing unto others what was done unto them" in that they have never seen what a truly trustworthy or caring parenting looks or feels like.

Their untrustworthiness can range all over the map of dysfunctionality, viciousness, exploitation, boundary-violation, sneaky sadism, sexual abuse, physical violence, "what you sees is *not* what you get," chaos, self-destructiveness, unpredictability, and on and on.

"POSSESSIVE" PARENTING PATTERN

"Don't *ever* leave me!" Their prime consideration is to do whatever is necessary to prevent the younger person from ever being able to leave and live successfully in the world.

To accomplish this end, which is usually unconscious, they will program the individual to be obnoxious, they will undermine the individual's competence and derail their development, they will over-"special"-ize the individual, they will train the person to act as their "action arm" in destructive ways, and they will do whatever else it takes to accomplish their intended final "tie that grinds" outcome.

They are, of course, either enamored of the individual, or totally dependent on them out of a profound sense of insufficiency on their part, or both.

"POWER-FEARING" PARENTING PATTERN

"Don't touch that dial!" They are terrified of setting off World War III if they or anyone in their vicinity impacts the environment. They come from a severely accusatory and reactive family.
****

"Potency-undermining." They are desperately afraid of losing their support system child(ren) if they own their potency, so they systematically frighten them from doing so. It comes from being so confidence-undermined that they feel utterly dependent upon their child(ren) to survive.

"POWER-PARANOIA-INDUCING" PARENTING PATTERN

"Don't let them see you!" They are terrified of responsibility, of potency, and of the requirements of life, and they pass this on to their child(ren) via contagion, example, precept and enforcement.

It is a pattern that got started in an upbringing that resulted in their feeling totally unprepared to handle the rigors of living life. They just want to "do their thing," with no restrictions, requirements or responsibilities.

"POWER-TRIPPING" PARENTING PATTERN

"You *vill* do vat I say!" They are totally into domination, control and determination of every outcome. They intend to make their child(ren) dance to their tune completely -- or else. They are the product of an authoritarian patriarchal household.

"PREOCCUPIED/SELF-IMMERSED" PARENTING PATTERN

"Trapped in the past." They are in effect unable to relate to the moment or to people, due to their being caught up in experiencing everything as a re-run of their childhood experiences.

As a result, they are ambivalent, inconsistent and ambiguous in their interpersonal and parenting relationships. They are the product of a similar family culture.

"PRIMITIVE" PARENTING PATTERN

"Cave ages." They operate in a very simple and simplistic manner, reacting from the gut and with intensely physical interventions. It arises from either an early soul development level and/or an equally primitive family history.

"PSEUDO-LOVING" PARENTING PATTERN

"Going through the motions." They continuously put out superficial displays of commitment to their child(ren) that are not matched by their underlying feelings and motivations. It is often reflective of a great deal of rageful resentment about their own unloving and passive-aggressive but untouchable-intangible rejection experience in childhood.

"PSEUDO-SPOUSE" PARENTING PATTERN

"Now YOU'RE the man/woman of the house!" They turn to their child(ren) to fill the needs that their absent or ineffective spouse doesn't fulfill, or that they won't allow them to fulfill -- often including the erotic arena, at least on the emotional level.

They were so incapacitated in the intimacy sphere that they can't handle adult peer spousal relationships.

"PUER/PUELLA" PARENTING PATTERN

"Dear Prudence." They in effect want a playmate, not the responsibilities of caring for and raising their own child(ren). They have never grown up, and they want to remain forever young, and they are using their child(ren) as the means to keep the delusion going.

They were of course prevented from maturing as a child by under-requiring and interference-running parenting.

"PUSHOVER" PARENTING PATTERN

"Complete capitulation." They feel unable to cope with the demands of life and their child(ren), and they cave in whenever any form of pressure is applied. They were massively undermined in confidence and competence as a child.

"REJECTING" PARENTING PATTERN

"Get out of my life!" Their experience is that their child(ren) are a nuisance, an irrelevance or revulsion, and they act on it. It arises from never having had any form of support or acceptance themselves.

"REPRESSIVE" PARENTING PATTERN

"Don't even think about it!" They run their life in a repression-dominated manner, and they enforce it with all the ferocity of survival threat reactions. And in the process, they model for and shape their child(ren) to do as they do. They are the product of a similar family system, and the beat goes on.

"RESCUE-TRIPPING" PARENTING PATTERN

"Interference-running." They are systematically intervening in their child(ren)'s life in such a manner as to prevent their developing the capacity for independent functioning. They are so dependent and/or passive-aggressively resentful that they can't do anything else.

They are the product of a severely dysfunctional family in which much of great untowardness happened, from which they have never recovered.

"RESENTFUL" PARENTING PATTERN

"If it weren't for you!" They feel that they are tied down, destiny-prevented, and enjoyment-derailed by their child(ren). They are the product of a similar family system, and they are passing it on.

"RESPECTFULNESS-AVOIDANT" PARENTING PATTERN

"Ruthless enviousness." They regard their child(ren) as "life supply competitors," and they'll be damned if they will let them get ahead of them in anything. They therefore withhold all expressions of support and respect in a ferociously authoritarian and competitive manner.

They are the product of a similar family culture.

"RESPONSIBILITY-AVOIDANT" PARENTING PATTERN

"Let George do it!" They systematically eschew any sorts of requirements, restrictions and responsibilities, including those connected with their child(ren). They absolutely hate to be demanded of or prevented in any way.

They are the product of an over-indulgent, under-requiring and supremely convenience-concerned parenting pattern.

"RESTRICTIVE" PARENTING PATTERN

"You'd better watch your P's and Q's!" They keep a very tight rein on any and all activities of their child(ren). To them, control is all-important, out of a deep distrust of the world.

They come from an untrustworthy and distrust-inducing experiential history.

"REVERSED ROLE" PARENTING PATTERN

"Emotional regression." The parent(s) in effect return to infancy/childhood, instead of "recapitulating" ("back burner remembering" what it was like at the same point in their own development, as nature's way of seeking to prevent the "passing on" of the worst of what happened).

They then expect their child(ren) to be THEIR parent at the deep emotional level. They have a "Take care of me!" approach to life, with the attitude and behavior pattern of one who feels both outclassed and overwhelmed, on the one hand, and they have the right to demand assistance and privilege, on the other.

They are the product of significantly depriving, convenience-concerned and/or damaging parenting.

"RIGHT AND RIGHTEOUS" PARENTING PATTERN

"It's God's *law!*" They are totally convinced that they know the one and only RIGHT way to do everything, and they consider it their responsibility to see to it that their child(ren) learn that way every minute of the day. They of course brook no interference or resistance, due to the "Divine Right of Parents" in these matters.

They are the product of a similar family background.

"RIGHT TO KILL" PARENTING PATTERN

"Right hand of God." They are convinced that the world is a highly dangerous and grossly evil place, in which it is their job to protect themselves and theirs, and to enforce the moral order. They are totally willing to go to any extremes in these undertakings.

They are, of course, passing it on from what they lived through as a child.

"RITUAL ABUSE" PERPETRATOR; "RITUALLY ABUSING" PARENTING PATTERN

"Diabolical monster." They are systematically slyly sadistic, and they are a subtly extremely violent and primitive soul who is consumingly hate-filled and evil-worshipping, in a violence-addicted (and increasing intensity-requiring), and dissociative manner (so that they don't feel the magnitude of what they are doing).

They are only concerned with getting their "hits," and with making absolutely sure they don't get caught. They are virulently vicious and utterly unprincipled in their pursuit of organized total depravity, ritualized torture and murder, cannibalism, gothically terrorizing and sexual destruction of children.

They are into seeking indications of ABSOLUTE ownership of children, adults and the behavior of those around them, and basing their activities on the assumed principles of Satanism, they go for complete control and degradation of everything and everyone that God loves (and Satan hates).

Their entire commitment is to bringing this about, and like "The Terminator," they could care less about the "current batch of fools" who are "trying to hold on to the old irrelevant and ridiculous ways."

They are often multigenerational, extending back for centuries of underground activity while carrying on normal-appearing lives on the surface. When they are not from such a background, they were forced into the process as a child, or they were so unthinkably abused and degraded that they were attracted to the ritual abuse group as an adult.

In any case, they are so damaged and deranged at the deep level that thus far, there is no treatment or effective handling of them, and they are unbelievably dangerous, as they delight in devising new and more torturous ways of keeping their secrets and of carrying out their inconceivable orgies.

Their motivation is the complete destruction of the positively motivated system, and the replacement of it with total take-over by pseudo-Satanic values and processes (which are horrifically hostile).

In terms of the underlying dynamics of this pattern, it is in essence a massively obsessional fixation on the fiendishly sadistic treatment that they underwent, starting with gothically hostile reactions to them in the womb.

They have identified with the aggressor, and they subject their victims to all the horrors of intra-uterine, birth process and infant period ghastly traumas that they experienced.

Their methods all involve highly sophisticated utilizations of torture technology, hypnosis, hysteria-induction, and mind-destroying extremities of experience.

"RIVALROUS" PARENTING PATTERN

"Everyone for themselves!" They treat their child(ren) as if they were competitors for the insufficient life support systems available for the family. It arises out of a similar experience in their childhood.

"ROLE-REVERSING" PARENTING PATTERN

"Emotional regression." The parent(s) in effect return to infancy/childhood, instead of "recapitulating" ("back burner remembering" what it was like at the same point in their own development, as nature's way of seeking to prevent the "passing on" of the worst of what happened).

They then expect their child(ren) to be THEIR parent at the deep emotional level. They have a "Take care of me!" approach to life, with the attitude and behavior pattern of one who feels both outclassed and overwhelmed, on the one hand, and that they have the right to demand assistance and privilege, on the other.

They are the product of significantly depriving, convenience-concerned and/or damaging parenting.

"RUG-YANKING" PARENTING PATTERN

"Trap-door-ing." They are forever suddenly devastatingly withdrawing support, resources, validation, follow-through and trustworthiness on their child(ren), as a function of self-immersed selfishness and/or relentless revenge-rage.

It is a pattern born of vicious malicious parenting in their childhood.

"SADISTIC" PARENTING PATTERN

"Doing unto others what was done unto them." They are "passing it on" to the next generation, because by the very nature of the syndrome, there is nothing else they can do. They are into total domination and torturing of their charges as a "mastery" strategy.

Of course, they are the product of the same syndrome in their family, and the beat goes on.

"SCARCITY ASSUMPTION" PARENTING PATTERN

"If you win, I lose." They operate as if there is not enough to go around, and that every gain by their child(ren) is their loss. So they go into "competition to the death" with their child(ren), in which they seek to hoard and control every ounce of sustenance in the family's environment.

It comes from a similar background, and they are definitely passing it on.

"SEDUCTIVE-DESTRUCTIVE" PARENTING PATTERN

"Passing it on." They are the product of super-seductive, "seduce-slap," "tantalizing tarantula" or frankly incestual parenting, and they are "doing unto others what was done unto them."

"SEEN BUT NOT HEARD" PARENTING PATTERN

"The less we hear from you the better!" They are intensely control-oriented and authoritarian in their functioning, especially with their child(ren). They are the product of similar parenting.

"SELF-CHECK-MATING"-INDUCING PARENTING PATTERN

"You do and you'll be so-o-o-o-ry!" When they were an infant and they started to engage in self-determining behavior, their mother warned of imminent annihilation, thereby harnessing all of the individual's resources for self-suppression, with a minimum of effort and no competence required of her.

It arises in her out of her feeling totally outclassed and overwhelmed by the child(ren). She herself was subjected to a severely suppressive parenting pattern.

"SELF-DISGUST-INDUCING" PARENTING PATTERN

"Blame-boomerang." (Pointing their finger at their child(ren) and saying, "I just HATE that about you!" as they suddenly turn their finger of blame back on themselves.) They project all their own self-hatred for being the cause of all their severe dysfunctional problems onto their children, following a generations-long pattern.

"SELF-DISTRUST-INDUCING" PARENTING PATTERN

"Oh no you don't!" They react to their child(ren)'s emerging capabilities with paranoia, rejection and/or revulsion, and they generate an abiding self-distrust in them as a result.

It arises from a highly distrusting parenting pattern in their upbringing.

"SELF-IMMERSED" PARENTING PATTERN

"Perennial infant." They are caught up in an emotional developmental fixation at a very early age of formation, due to similar parenting.
****

"Lost in their own stuff." They are so self-involved that it has disrupted their functioning in a way that prevents them from being able to take into account external needs.

They were never given the support and training in living that they needed.

"SELFISH" PARENTING PATTERN

"What's in it for me?" They sort only on what pays off for them, with little or immersed and exploitative family. They are now passing it on to their child(ren).

SEXUAL ABUSE OF CHILD (Perpetrator)

"Misguided love." They are highly primitive in their emotional development, and they act out sexually towards those they feel love towards. They mean well, but they are severely inappropriate in their love expression.

They are the product of a maturity-undermining and severely dysfunctional family.
****

"Playing doctor." They are in effect an emotional peer of their victim, and they are in effect playing with them and/or expressing their affection in a highly inappropriate manner.

They are an emotional child who never got past middle childhood in their emotional development, due to severely invasive mothering. At times, this can be a very loving but hopelessly inadequate fathering situation.

They were systematically undermined and infantilized as a child, and they have in effect never gotten out of childhood.
****

"Desperately seeking Susan." She is putting the child in their parent/God/spouse position in an emotional starvation and worth-deprivation reaction. They are trying to heal the devastating impact of severe maternal deprivation, followed by paternal rejection.
****

"I can't stop myself!" They become "possessed" in a dissociative and/or an overwhelmingly motivated manner. It is a pattern that got started in their severely sex-ploitative, denial-dominated, suppressive and dysfunctional family.
****

"It's my right!" They are doing unto others what was done unto them, either helplessly as their own pathology takes over or collusively or even proudly, as they manifest their devastating history.
****

"Doing unto others what was done unto her." They are on a vengeance-vendetta, along the lines of "Somebody's gonna PAY for this!" Their rage knows almost no limits, and the more damage they can see, they better it makes them feel.

It is the result of systematically sadistic parenting, in an "apprenticeship training" manner.
****

"Raging rapist." They have a vengeance/power-tripping mentality in which they are acting out their profound frustration over their effective powerlessness by "lording it over" the child.

It is the resultant of being treated as "special" by a sex-ploitative mother to such a degree that they are in effect derailed from their destiny, and they are out for blood.

"SEXUALIZING" PARENTING PATTERN

"Sexual object." They respond to their child(ren) as if they were an erotic toy for their enjoyment. They operate as if they have no awareness or caring about what that does to the child(ren). They are so self-immersed that they can only manifest what turns them on. It is the result of a similar family culture when they were a child.

SEXUALLY ABUSING PARENTING RELATIONSHIP DISORDER

"Objectifying." They are so self-immersed that they can only see their child(ren) as the means to their gratification or release. They are extremely distorted in their thinking, and they are narcissistically unable to be empathically responsive.

They were subjected to the same massive violations of their boundaries, and it thoroughly undid their capacity for compassion and commitment.

"SEXUALLY SATURATED" PARENTING PATTERN

"Pedestalizing parenting." They are totally infatuated with and erotically attracted to their child(ren), and they react by spoiling them and by depending abjectly upon them. They are so unsure of themselves as a result of severe competence-undermining parenting that they can't relate to an adult peer intimately, so they turn to their child.

"SEXUAL REJECTION" PARENTING PATTERN

"You *WHAT!!??*" They systematically reject their child(ren) around their sexuality and their gender. It is reflective of their rejection and intense fear of their own sexuality and gender that was generated by severely rejecting and suppressive parenting in their childhood.

"SHADOW-SHOVING" PARENTING PATTERN

"Speak no evil!" They are intensely fearfully denial-dominated in their functioning and in their family culture. It is a resultant of severe fear of what would emerge if they got in touch with their underside.

They grew up in a ferociously suppressive family.

"SHAME-INDUCING" PARENTING PATTERN

"Aren't you ashamed of yourself!?" They make their child(ren) feel as if they are somehow lacking in fundamental qualities, and as if they are in some way "evil" by their very nature.

In so doing, they are coming from a severe morally oriented pattern based on intense feelings of evilness in them, induced by their own parents.

SHARED PSYCHOTIC DISORDER ("Folie a deux" -- "craziness of two")

"Double-bubble ego." The child's parent is a paranoid who has an elaborated delusional system that has incorporated the child. The child assumes that reality is as their parent has indicated it, and they then carry out the psychosis as they live their life. OR the child transfers the pattern in full bloom to a stand-in for their parent in later life, as they pass it on.

"SIBLING RIVALRY-ENCOURAGING" PARENTING PATTERN

"Fight over it!" The parents hold themselves back and they dispense favors to their various children in a rivalry-abetting fashion so as to have power and to have commitment coming their way from their children.

They come from a scarcity-emphasizing background.

"SMOTHERING BUT COLD" MOTHERING

"Engulfing glacier." They impose their will and their intention to keep the child(ren) around the old homestead, but they have no ability to be available or to be emotionally responsive or concerned.

They were "left out in the cold" as a child, and they are not about to have it happen again.

"SMOTHER-MOTHERING"

"Mama knows best!" They approach everything in an "eternal maternal" manner. They tend to have a "chicken soup" model of everything, and they are guilt-dominated and guilt-inducing, in a wrong-making pattern.

It is the resultant of having had to take over the maternal role in their dysfunctional family.

"SNEAKY SADIST" PARENTING PATTERN

"Passing it on." They are a subtly vicious malicious vengeance-vendetta in action, and they are subjecting their child(ren) to it intensively. They are also "apprenticing" at least one of their children.

It is a pattern that goes back for generations.

"SOUL-SEARING" PARENTING PATTERN

"Twisto-flex thinking." They distort realities in such a way as to "mind-screw," "deviantly self-justify," and devastatingly damage. They effectively convince everyone that their child(ren) are "moral monsters."

It works by so permanently scarring their child(ren)'s inner core by the events that result and/or by the impact and import of what they are imprinted into "buying" as a result of their brilliant mental gymnastics and meaning manipulations.

It is a pattern that results from supremely self-immersed and subtly evil parents because of their ultimate impact on the world. In other words, they are passing on a generations old "tradition."

"SPECIAL"-TREATING PARENTING PATTERN

"You are the total cat's meow and the world will- red carpet you!" They have become totally enamored of their child(ren), and they give them anything they want, and they constantly give them things, as they never-endingly make over their child(ren). They are too immature to be able to have an adult peer intimate relationship, and they have totally invested in one child as their spouse.

They were treated in such a way as a child as to prevent their ever becoming competent and confident enough to function as an adult.

"SPOILING" PARENTING PATTERN

"Anything you want, dearest!" They give their child(ren) everything they ask for and more. It arises out of convenience-concern, out of fear of rejection or abandonment, and/or it may have a hidden hostility behind it.

In any case, they are supremely self-immersed due to an incompetence parenting pattern in their childhood.

"SPOUSE-SUBSTITUTE" PARENTING PATTERN

"You're the (wo)man in my life!" They have turned their child(ren) into their mate(s), often involving severe sex-ploitation or sexual saturation, perhaps even with sexual abuse. They were thoroughly damaged by their family to such a degree that they can't sustain or maintain a true peer-peer relationship with an adult.

"SQUABBLING SIBLINGS" PARENTING PATTERN

"Two kids." In effect, two developmentally "flat-lined" children got married, and then they carried on their "sibling rivalry" lifestyle into their parenting responsibilities.

They are the product of a competence-undermining, self-immersed, and/or dysfunctional family.

"TANTALIZING TARANTULA" PARENTING PATTERN

"Seduce-slap." They continuously do seductive-destructive erotic "game-playing" on their child(ren). It is a form of psychological incest in which the child is constantly promised love via erotic stimulation, and then they are slammed up against the wall moralistically for responding to the proffered "love."

It is of course a matter of passing it on -- doing unto others what was done unto them.

"THEY CAN DO NO RIGHT" PARENTING PATTERN

"What have you done NOW!?" Their focus is continually on what is wrong with everything, especially with their child(ren). They are unable to see what is right about things, and they feel constantly beset by fiendishly mean developments, and they feel surrounded by a "ship of fools."

They are the product of severely wrong-making parenting.

"THEY CAN DO NO WRONG" PARENTING PATTERN

"My little darling(s)." They operate out of the delusion that their child(ren) are the epitome of perfection. Their child(ren) are their ego extensions, and they become an infuriated mother bear if anyone dares to impugn them for their continuously spoiled and ecologically unconcerned behavior.

They were severely narcissistically wounded by their uncaring and self-immersed parents.

"TIE THAT GRINDS" PARENTING PATTERN

"You're mine!" They have the total conviction at the gut level that their child(ren) are their exclusive property, and they respond with rage at the fact that their child(ren) intend to have a life of their own. They fight back with severe enmeshing, guilt-inducing and even life-threatening tactics.

It is the resultant of never having had their emotional needs met as a child, and it often is a situation of "passing it on."

"TORTURING" PARENTING PATTERN

"Righteous viciousness." They systematically subject their child(ren) to massively punitive and sadistic treatment, out of a belief that they deserve it. It arises from having been similarly treated as a child.

"TRIPOD-RAGE"-INDUCING PARENTING PATTERN

"Men are the cause of all evils." They implant and/or inculcate an abiding rage, disgust and distrust of males, men and the patriarchy in their daughter, starting during the symbiotic period of infancy.

They are passing on what happened to them.

"TRIPOD-RAGE" PARENTING PATTERN

"Just like your father!" They carry their fulminating fury at the patriarchy and at the male gender into their parenting of their male child(ren), with massively crippling and often "Goodbar-rage"-generating results.

"UGLY DUCKLING-INDUCING" PARENTING PATTERN

"What are YOU doing here!?" They are overwhelmed, alarmed and disgusted by the potency and superiority of their child(ren). They want no part of it, and they are determined that their child(ren) will not cause trouble by manifesting their capabilities.

They come from a suppressive, conformity-enforcing dysfunctional family, or they are doing unto others what was done unto them.

"UNCONCERNED" PARENTING PATTERN

"So . . .?" They are unresponsive and uninvolved with what is happening around them, particularly with their child(ren). They are the product of a numbingly destructive or unconcerned parenting pattern.

UNDER-INVOLVED PARENTING RELATIONSHIP DISORDER

"Nobody home." They are in effect emotionally not here, and they are lost in their own world and concerns. They are unable to be really concerned about, much less to be able to meet their child(ren)'s needs.

No one was ever there for them either, and they are developmentally very primitive in their functioning.

"UNDER-REQUIRING" PARENTING PATTERN

"Convenience-concerned." They are more involved in their immediate comforts than in what the longer range consequences of their parenting pattern are. They are themselves the product of severely self-immersed parenting.
****

"Keep them around the old homestead." They are afraid of alienating their child(ren) or allowing their child(ren) to grow away, so they don't impose even the requirements of community living on them.

They are the product of an enmeshed possessive family, and they are just "passing it on."

"UNIMPORTANT" PARENTING PATTERN

"*What* kids?" They treat their child(ren) as being insignificant and as being very low on their list of priorities in life. They are simply passing on what was done unto them.

"UNPREDICTABLE" PARENTING PATTERN

"You never know . . ." They live a chaotic and dysfunctional lifestyle that results in high uncertainty about how far things might go and what kind of things might happen.

They come from a similar family background.

"UNTRUSTWORTHY" PARENTING PATTERN

"Hidden and nefarious agendas." They brought with them severe baggage from their own childhood around vengeance, righteousness, gaminess, dysfunctionality and ragefulness.

"VAST WASTELAND" PARENTING PATTERN

"Running on empty." There is a great deal of deprivation and insufficiency in their family, a pattern that got started in a severely sparse childhood.

VERBALLY ABUSIVE PARENTING RELATIONSHIP DISORDER

"I can't handle it!" They feel utterly overwhelmed by their child, and they have the unconscious experience that the child is doing it to them in a sadistically and/or rejectingly negative attack.

They are acting out their own massive self-rejection resulting from similar parenting.

"VICIOUS-MALICIOUS" PARENTING PATTERN

"Vengeance is mine!" They are extracting a pound of flesh for every ounce of misery they have experienced. They systematically subject their children to subtle, sly, subterranean sabotage and treacherous torture. They are simply passing on what was done unto them. Often it is completely unconscious and unobservable.

It is the resultant of equally virulent vengeance-vendetta parenting in their own childhood.

"VIOLENT" PARENTING PATTERN

"WHERE *IS* S/HE!?" They react to any frustration, presumed insubordination or less than expected performance with a raging and physically explosive response that includes violence.

They are a very primitive personality who never got beyond the "terrible two" period of emotional/social development because of capitulating or "action arm exploitative" parenting.

"WHAT'S IN IT FOR ME?" PARENTING PATTERN

"My servant(s)." They are heavily convenience-concerned and self-serving, with their child(ren) being regarded and treated as resources and support systems who have no real right to make demands.

They are passing on what happened to them in a "doing unto others what was done unto them" pattern.

"WHAT WILL THE NEIGHBORS THINK?" PARENTING PATTERN

"Appearances first!" They live their life in terms of social acceptability and rejection-avoidance, and they impose this regimen on their children ferociously. It comes from having been reared with perfectionistic performance requirements.

"WHY DON'T YOU DO THE WORLD A FAVOR AND GO PLAY ON THE FREEWAY?" PARENTING PATTERN

"I can't take one more thing!" They have total intolerance of any more demands and responsibilities than those involved in barely surviving and fending off the next disaster.

They are the product of a totally demoralizingly chaotic and devastatingly destructive dysfunctional family. The result is they have just enough energy and consciousness available to handle the next crisis, period.

Anything more is reacted to in a "blindly slashing out" manner.

****

"I *hate* this!" They are parenthood-hating and/or total rejecting of a particular child -- they can't handle the fact that the child exists in their life. It is a pattern that comes out of a massively destructive dysfunctional childhood that resulted in their being supremely self-immersed, disgusted, disdainful and detached from anything but the immediate experiential value of whatever is happening.

They look no farther than the end of their nose, because they were never allowed to do so in their "upbringing."

"WILL OF SPAGHETTI" PARENTING PATTERN

"Overwhelmed." They feel completely up against the wall at all times. And they are particularly blown out by the requirements of child-rearing. They were totally demoralized and cope-ability-destroyed by their massively chaotic and dysfunctional family.

"WILL-O'-THE-WISP" PARENTING PATTERN

"Hope-hooking." They systematically tantalize their child(ren) with the promise of "nirvana" and the "God Housekeeping Seal of Approval" if the child(ren) rise to ever unspecified standards of manifestation.

It has the effect of prolonging the "in loco Deity" effect (where children put God's face on their parents till they are about three or four) indefinitely, with the result that their child(ren) never can connect or commit anywhere else. It is, of course, a "passing it on" pattern. ("Nirvana" is fusion with God.)

"WIPE THAT SMILE OFF YOUR FACE, YOUNG MAN/LADY!" PARENTING PATTERN

"Brooks no interference." They operate a "tight little ship," they will tolerate no independence or noncompliance, and they react with violence to anything that strikes them as potential insubordination.

They are the product of a similar family system.

"WITHDRAWING" PARENTING PATTERN

"Disaster-deflecting." Every time things get close to them or that things start to matter to them, they withdraw from the fray. It arises from feeling completely incapable of handling vulnerability and involvement, due to never having experienced any sort of closeness with their family. Indeed, their experience was that vulnerability is disaster.

"WITHHOLDING" PARENTING PATTERN

"Staying on top." They systematically deny their children validation, involvement and emotional support out of an underlying fear of losing control of the situation.

They are very fearful of intimacy, due to deeply distrust-inducing parenting.

"WRONG-MAKING" PARENTING PATTERN

"Do it RIGHT, dammit!" They have deep-seated resentment and/or perfectionistic expectations that result in their responding to every move the child makes that doesn't fit their desires with wrong-making and anger.

It is a pattern that got started from a similar experiential history as a child.

2006 Dr. Lincoln decided to revise and expand all of his works. We are pleased to present you his est revised work. See our website www.talkinghearts.net for the latest information on releases.

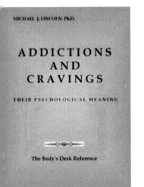

Addiction and Cravings: Their Psychological Meaning (1991, Rev. 2006)

This book is an outstanding overview on the nature of Addictions and Cravings. In addition, a "Dictionary" of the Psychological (and occasionally the sacred) meanings of various addictions and cravings ranging from "Crack" to Mozart. Spiral Bound, 369 pages

Retail $69.00

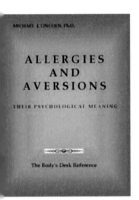

Allergies and Aversions: Their Psychological Meaning (1991, Rev. 2006)

Allergies and Aversions A dictionary of the psychological dynamics and learning history underlying 300 of the most common allergies is presented for the purposes of understanding the meaning of having an intolerance response to these substances. Spiral Bound, 123 Pages

Retail $34.00

What's in a Face? (1990, Rev. 2007)
The "Dictionary" for Heart Centered Face Reading
An exhaustive dictionary of the psychological (and occasionally the sacred) meanings of facial structure, including head characteristics and hair qualities. It coalesces the ancient Chinese system for doing this is called "Siang Mien" (pronounced SEE-ahng MEE-un), which means "investigating spirit." The contents of this dictionary include the utilizable contents of Siang Mien, plus the best of the West and the author's own experiences over the last 40 years of study of this subject. Spiral binding, 273 pages

Retail $59.00

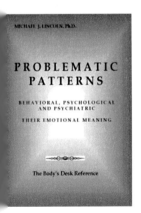

Problematic Patterns (1991, Rev. 2007)
Behavioral, Psychological and Psychiatric Their Emotional Meanings
A brief discussion of the nature of Problematic Patterns of personal and behavioral functioning, followed by a "dictionary" of a considerable number of patterns, including the psychiatric diagnostic system, Michael J. Lincoln's diagnostic system, the enneagram point problems, the deadly sins, numerous traits and many, many more patterns. Using the DSM's as a benchmark you will find items like Drama Triangle-Addict, Compulsive Disorders, Perfectionism and Stress-Seeking Patterns to name a few. Comb binding, 799 pages

Retail $149.00

Visit our website to Order www.talkinghearts.net

Honey, I Blew Up the Kids! (1992, Rev. 2007)
Comprehensive approach to Parenting
An in-depth exploration of the issues, parameters, and experiences of parenting. Also provided is a comprehensive approach to parenting based on realistic, vital awareness and values also explore the dictionary on problematic parenting patterns. Learn how to parent the soul, deal with an old soul child, Indigo/Crystal children as well. Spiral binding, 149 pages

Retail $36.00

WHAT'S HAPPENING TO ME!!?? (1981, Rev. 2007)
A Road Map to the Journey of Change and the Healing Process
This book is about what happens when you reach a place where it is necessary to reconstruct yourself. The idea is to get an overview of what the various events in this process mean. It has the effect of clarifying this process so that it's not so confusing, demoralizing, enraging, and alarming. It also has the effect of accelerating the healing process when you have some sort of understanding of What's Happening to you. Spiral Binding, 139 Pages

Retail $34.00

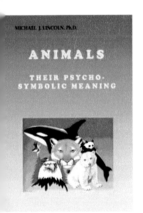

Animals Their Psycho-Symbolic Meaning (1991, Rev. 2007)
A discussion of the nature of animals as symbols in our society and how to interpret them. The ways in which they appear in our lives, the sources of their significance, and the types of indications involved. This leads into a dictionary of the archetypic symbolic and psychological meanings of over 500 animals. Also discussed are the varieties of symbolic meaning in the literature, along with the nature of the purposes of the animal's entering your life at this time.
Spiral binding, 490 pages

Retail $79.00

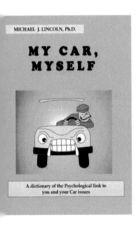

My Car, Myself (1991, Rev. 2008)
A dictionary of the psychological meanings of having your car break down with regard to what the breakdowns indicate about what is happening for you at the time, as a kind of early warning system. It covers most of the major components of the car, ranging from the fuel pump to the floor mats. It also interprets other aspects of your relationship with your car, such as driving habits, traffic tickets, disruptive behaviors and car attitudes It actually works!
Spiral binding, 305 pages

Retail $59.00